TRUTH SURREAL
AND THE
ADMONISHMENT

TRUTH SURREAL AND THE ADMONISHMENT

JOSHUA JOSEPH

TATE PUBLISHING
AND ENTERPRISES, LLC

Published by Tate Publishing & Enterprises, LLC
127 E. Trade Center Terrace | Mustang, Oklahoma 73064 USA
1.888.361.9473 | www.tatepublishing.com

Tate Publishing is committed to excellence in the publishing industry. The company reflects the philosophy established by the founders, based on Psalm 68:11,
"The Lord gave the word and great was the company of those who published it."

Book design copyright © 2013 by Tate Publishing, LLC. All rights reserved.

Published in the United States of America

ISBN: 978-1-63063-765-1
1. Poetry / General
2. Poetry / American / General
13.11.18

To the prophets, freaks and poets

Contents

Part One

TRUTH SURREAL

SECRET LOVE TRAPPED IN A SUB FOLDER

I could not say who or where I am
Though her whisper made me absolute and sure-
She speaks from far out at sea, the waters carry her words like the winds carry the birds
My ears tuned by the shepherd musician; with herbs, wisdom and a harp, a bond was formed-
I can hear her through many storms telling me to keep an ear to the sea- to confess she makes me wise-

I would have her come by now for I am already wiser than the tolerance of other men can bear
So to sit with vacant heart and listen,
For she continues to place gems of knowledge round my brown neck, serving to be envied and hated-

Knowing nothing of her profound wisdom would render me with an empty speech of love and longing, become easily overlooked and would have no good thing to offer men, in return they would offer me a fine friendship, for the minds of simple men are eager to recruit indifferent supporters for their conscience's sake.

Many nights I envisioned her walking, contradicting the movement of the sun as a creature of lore following the broken star as it falls toward my fate and hers, as it falls she walks on the surface of the waves, they are as cooled sand to her, the dunes at midnight but with the reflection of water, the sea looks up at long legs stretching nautical miles, all the permanently set stars fixed in the cement of the night sky look down and out of the sea like teeming schools of cod, like the eyes of many neurotic Pharaohs who have sacrificed their souls for the dream of space, I have my soul at the cliff's edge awaiting a fatal love to summon me to leap-

I see all of this but not once has been the time of our meeting, no, only whispers of meaning attached to that which is perceived.

Someone must make her aware of my deferred hope; from Norway the many brave who travel by way of the wind, the captains with many strong rowers at their command, Jonah please agree to speak and thou will be vomited from the belly of the whale, even one of a thousand sailing merchants could tell her when rounding the ports for the sale of silk, fine oils and whatever else Babylon deems desirable, all or anyone who travels the lowest parts of the earth; the high seas. Tell her to come... or to be quiet for I can no longer accept the sound of secret love.

CISTERNS

A galaxy has given birth to day
This page a threshing floor, this pen a winnowing fork
My companions are dukes and grand duchesses
Fate; one tenth of Melchizedek's decision
Plato has read aloud to me the Republic
Within my hand a book, its parchments reflect the life I took
Catherine the Great Wall has fallen
Release the spirit of Abaddon
For the Day of Atonement is nearing
Meet me in the Josaphat Valley
For the temple has long been obsolete
For three years I warned with tears
For day and night I warned with tears
Two evils they have committed
So their cisterns can hold no water.

HAVE YOURSELF

Have yourself a merry little Christmas-

The song played over the radio; in forward motion my mind began to slip into a gear contrary to the transmission of my automobile, I gave allowance for the truck to become as a leaf, no, rather a single page of newspaper; for in the city it is the words and thoughts of man that litter the sidewalks-

Grace was given to me as I paid nothing in the form of attention to my speed, traffic, painted lines- stop signs, yield signs or any color variation of an overhead lamp- no, I was driving under the influence, so I must not apologize for giving a true account, well, aside from this.. I am sorry-

Now then- Oblivious to reasonable- routine- sensibilities of operating a motor vehicle I was instead engrossed with faces and a concept; a concept possibly looming in all of our minds, all at the same time of day, no matter who I looked upon there was an overwhelming possibility that they were perhaps having very similar thoughts as their beholder- if I told you I was merely reflecting you would not truly share in imagining the spell- even in the most serene Tibetan temple, the most quiet hill on Zion, you would not share in the truth of the moment, you would most commonly rest on the notion of a self imposed moment of intrigue- to avoid this misunderstanding, this trampling of pearls, I will tell you that apart from their supposed expectation,.. I breathed of their pain, their sorrow- and with that you must attempt to be compassionate.

The song led me to a startling acclamation for itself, I thought; this song, it has gay, cheery sentiments and yet the melody is as melancholy as Chopin's Nocturnes- it was at this that I wondered if the creator of one of the most well known holiday jingles knew what he had done, or if this was the very meaning of what he had done, the only reason it played so long before it be dammed from my perceiving was on account of being carried into this state I had found myself in, it then entered in sat down and was right at home, destiny is sometimes fulfilled in the mind- so there it was perfectly accompanying my thought pattern. The sentiment of Christmas in word and deed with a dark shadow of sultry reality, a mournful expression of truth filing into the holiday greeting card- like- "merry Christmas and a new year just like the last 15"- we enjoy a holiday because the rest of every day thereafter is misery or work, or... work- no not for everybody, not for me or for you, just everyone else, everyone who is not going to receive this trump to digest.

I thought first of folks I knew personally, those unhappy and unsatisfied, I thought; for them this backdrop of celebration is a kick to the gut... except they can't gasp for air in front of anyone, they have to excuse themselves to the restroom, look into the mirror, look into the last 40 years and face the face that is older, colder and less likely to smile candidly at its own surprise, as the worst comes to the surface just under the skin and tightens at the neck, the eruption of guilt, remorse and regret translates into tears- a ruffled chin and a sense to quiet the sadness once more, even though the sounds of mourning could no way be heard over the gleeful motion outside the bathroom door- over the sink a sob is released and then washed down with soap and running water, the sound of running water comforts the one in direst and that one is reminded that all will pass and one day be no more and that may be just fine enough.

As I traveled through time and place I looked upon brothers and sisters unknown, looking deep into each of their faces, The Ghost held the sun still, I floated before them... incredibly slow, watched as each step brought about a drip of consideration to the forefront of their being, turning wheels of existence, consciousness,.. I can see them even now- cars circling an intersection, each burning the fuels of mother earth to meet a deadline, to secure a Christmas morning, the world does seem to work in its own maddening way, like a mutant organism, out of pure necessity...surviving- anyway, there she was on the corner, looking and scheming, how would she get across? She was overweight, wearing a white bandanna, her skin dark black, she walked, two steps then back, two steps then over to the side, trying to keep her momentum but there was pain, she leaned left onto her leg then shot upright grinding her teeth, one leg weak, a hip ridden with discomfort but she goes on, we all go on and on adapting,.. or do we? Sure we do but our minds and hearts are troubled nonetheless- she knew it was Christmas... but it hurt just the same.

Three brothers step out of a Plymouth Horizon, yellow, hatchback- you probably don't know the car- brothers because they belong to one nation, one ghetto. The ghettos are always there to say exactly what we do when we have a chance, likewise it says exactly what we do when there is no chance at all- scaffolding is set before a decaying store front, others have chosen to hang clothes from the yellow, tubular steel, either to dry or sell either or it exemplifies the manipulation of an environment. A road will bring you through the heart of principalities and powers, seeing the zombies, the wolves, the serpents and doves- the injured- afflicted- the fathers and grandfathers passing down the urban demeanor, the lean and swank with each street step the fermentation of pain and bondage-

An aesthetic of its own-

What does this have to do with Christmas-- this is Christmas - these are Christmas- down market past the district- just keep going, even further than 32nd- the days belong to the living- the thinking- the walking-

When I laugh merrily amongst the gluttonous stock of plenty, laughing, spinning, walking across to stockings filled with cold, green, reeking cash, I know within myself how utterly strange in fortune this would seem to one who lacks in the necessities of life- and so knowing this truth I must bear witness to it even as the present laughter rings in my ears,,,, my soul is aware of the polar fact.

What then do we say, eat drink and be merry for tomorrow we will die, no.... no

Have yourself a Merry Little Christmas... trust your children to sit on the lap of a strange big man with a long beard if for only once in a year, stretch and try to touch the phenomenon of a national holiday, whether you are in love with it, trying to get over it or just plain acting like it doesn't exist.... you are a part of this, this Christmas, for to me it is nothing and yet I lie, for how could something be nothing, no it is marvelous, a marvelous phenomenon of commonality, something to everyone whether you like it or not here it is.

So I am fascinated, fascinated by strangers and family, by life and the hand a certain holiday plays in it, we are helpless to discover our reflection in that mirror, truly we walk away forgetting what we look like, knowing it will return but yet not for some time and we will once again measure our happiness, our maturity and our compassion before a great many witnesses some known and some forgotten-

So have yourself a merry little Christmas-

YOU MY FAWN

Perhaps a wreath will cover your incandescent iniquity
Their praise mute the Almighty
Escape the sentence of truth
Do you think
Beseeching the showman to go on
The women to recline
Pogo stick lips streaming contemptible encouragement
Wise blows were too painful for this generation
Let's face it
Get wasted
For you
There's only ever been you
Except at the receptions of America
Like... Kwanzaa or Christmas
Quiet, I'm reading you might scare the stimuli
Don't cry if only for my attention span deary
Once departed I will just ask those fans within my cup
Listen child; put your ear to the porcelain
Innumerable cheers from the tiny hearts of a quantum specie
A city is precisely a civilization
My composition is almost through
You my fawn will be the choicest of figures

PHILIDELPHIA

All the hugs
What's ups
handshakes
fake graces
flakes of human communions
styles illusions
running, running, running
cops have gang ego
how they betrayed thought and the thinker

COLD LEAVES

Cold wet leaves, a sob reminiscent of a child. I heard nothing and yet their words were many and somehow irreverent though they were most solemn men- we receive so many certifications- bleak parchment that certifies ones death, cursed morbid drawing is such-foolish act and proof for the franchise of the last breath- For it was the first time I smelled the death of human flesh.

I pictured him in a horizontal position, slowly rotating, constantly, three hundred and sixty degrees, higher and higher away from us, further and further into mystery, for he passed over the threshold from life to the unknown, unheard, unseen there after... whatever we knew or thought we knew of the man is even further from certainty and what was never understood passes deep and hides itself under Atlantis.

He is hearing us outside his door as he rotates he hears us together talking, he rotates and hears the days of mourning, the days of laughter, the days of communal reminiscing, and as it creeps to less and less he ascends and descends further and further away until he can hear no more, just as his name is seldom spoken-we are born, we die, they speak about our life, our death is documented, examined and others pick through all the extensions that distracted you all the days of your consumption, they search for answers but now the man is gone, to tell stories no more- just like that- for before this I have not smelled human death- our communities are more like catacombs- tombs of the lonely and forgotten- their parting day is kept hidden just as their prior days of living behind a door, under a tombstone, a house is a tomb- and now a haunting to encounter- much fear abounded on the front yard or side yard... it was all an unusual mess- stepping over wet cold leaves- approaching a man's shadowy abode... through the glass, silence, one lamp; a flashing screen harnessing false peace for all the lonely world to never be afraid when lit- fear gripped my reality likened to eight mm film with every step I recoiled- for I had never smelled human death before- my mind produced warning after warning, my life, I myself wanted to escape, to get far away from such a daunting realization of mortality- horror, it seems as nothing less than horror. He may have been lying there for days, for he was with no one, no one to carry out the man who had passed – creatures met him in the deathly fabrics of clothes and blankets, having no heart; eating the man whom I shook hands, exchanged expression and confronted difference, the difference within all human will- we are born, we die and someone has to look at your dead face, touch your lifeless body- the living has no choice but to face the death that awaits them- for I have never smelled human death- all seemed tainted, all seemed grim, death seemed partly attached to all life, only waiting to completely consume it- cursed man to die, cursed ground, is not all joy fleeting- the foul smell of death truly offends the living but the dead rotates further and further away- released from all- affected no more by no one- their temporal tent perishes as the inner fire awaits the judgment- a live dog is better than a dead lion- when living, one walks in opportunity but the fate of the dead is sealed by their last breath. The one born again, in this one life is highly defiant; though he dies... he lives.

THIRA

In any attempt to find solitude one most always seems to injure his company and finds that where he goes is ironically occupied- came to meet the edge of the sea, seems where all the stray dogs meet in Kamari- there I also met the hotel owner's son; dressed down with his teeth spotted brown- "this hotel you are staying in; this is my father's hotel," I replied- Emanuel it seems I am a guest in your father's house- I walked on promising we would speak again, he was not through telling me how much he hated the Turks. Oh Santorini I thought: you beautiful greedy women.

Santorini, Santorini- the skirt of Thira, many steps the men willingly climb- your breasts formed of the rock that faces the sea, no man chiseled, no descending drops of sweat.- Welcoming all who enter the world- The Philistine, Albanian, Greek. Santorinians the sun has welded you all into the cliff side, bronzed the same hue as the one who is stone- arrogant- I have only one true friend in this part of the world, the rest are proud, arrogant men-

Onto ancient Thira where the spirit of the land manifests its anger through the howling of the wind- for this steep mountainside leads only to desolate plateaus that have been long forgotten by her own and even longer ago thanked for the advantage of downward force and provident sight against any enemy that would approach from any four leadings of the wind, now it is left to be peacefully invaded again and again as travelers with heavy steps peer off to its many sides and clumsily walk upon the wide planks of Christendom; ignorant of the hymn- the candle- the water and the sand.

You Santorinians have left your greatest love for foreigners to tread and will most assuredly regret loving the port and the skirt of the goddess for though she is beautiful and causes all to place goods in your lap, even kings of Mesopotamia will be swallowed, when all are amused with her and I shall howl ever more past strangers on the mount of the true Thira- I am her- I am the true

Thira- I move this ground with shallow breath and with jealousy-
as you left me vacant- vacant you left my heart and center.
Developing further from my peak, with one accord you all
migrated, following one another, deciding for yourselves the prime
location to cast out ye nets upon the passing nations, you chose
where the tide would wash you up the collected purses. With
certain expectancy I saw all of my stewards, all of my passionate
shepherds lay down at once for the impermanent gain- you my
children, my foolish children thanked the sea and the naval- I- I-
the true Thira possessed- twas thine own naval, many, many great
men sought refuge in port and weathered, feeding their bellies as
the seas raged, yet their ships rocked as a fair Mediterranean child
in a mother's arms. You all accepted the bounty over and over
again- with each temptress pushing a mighty crew to port, I grew
more tense, the seas would rock against my broad bosom and
curved sides while the adultery at port went on merrily- I was filled
that day, full of fiery motion- you all forget even the question of
what could rise up against such a great fortress, such a wonder to
seamen- a gift- Santorinians you left your first love and used my
body to comfort your families, with all the heat invested within,
I released- destroying what you created of me- no more would
I keep out the seas- my body now three- the waves took up swell
and charged- swallowing all they could of me- consuming stone-
you were a mighty country rooted in the sea- now a province-
broken- floating stones- The saying is true; you are not people, you
are Santorinians-

Just as your land is not land- not part of the original creation-
From Hades you arose- from the middle of the sea-
You boiled and hardened-
I heard your crying sink deep, sinking deeper with my body to
the floor-
How could our lives taper as the ocean into the horizon
How could we just fade into silence, how do we now feel our
existence slipping away
You sank feeling the sting that swells the mind of a son losing
his father to the grave-
You cried with me alas- Mother Withhold Us from The Sea

MORE THAN

Took me so long to meet death
  Took me seven years to see
  A ghoul of the darkened hours
  I stood and watched the reflection of who I was fall slowly
  Almost forgetting the morbid time and time and time and a
half of licentious living
  He whispered a sort of warm breeze before us, always with us
then, as a muse, we were enchanted and
  Were together through the night when many are alone
  There was a feeling, how do I explain... strong seduction
  We believed the lie, yes, and were proud of it
  Armed with leather, plastic baggies and a reputation that
simply pounded through the night
  We were the night... and all it stood for
  Though, I did think, I thought a lot, thought how I could
become greater at each cheap shot
  Yet all the while I was led, thinking I was the wolf, a most
unholy ghost tempted me with the scent of blood- for power and
life are in the blood
  We were tight, nothing would end our glory, our glory and
our laughing would always be heard of
  Kings of cool, no one had to tell us for we all bore witness as
an evil fate brought us lower and lower
  Now it just seems as a dream I struggle to remember, you can
feel the dream but fail in discerning its source and reason, you are
simply driven through like a child, prior to receiving the knowledge
of your independent life
  When I was a child I thought like a child, now I am a man
  The gaze then was a horizon, early dawn, our silhouettes
darkening tomorrow, standing in our own way keeping one

another cold, kicking one another, shouting- GET UP, GET UP YOU PUSSY ITS NOT COLD.

We injured to make strong, to make head strong, to make bad strong... to make monsters out of boys, however our boyhood was now renounced for its innocence and weakness would only shame us in our endeavors... for I myself had something to forget, I am sure we all did, although it was not spoken of, it was as if we were all there for each other, gathered by a beast to be fattened and slaughtered

I would stare into the abyss for hours and hours, it soon became days, I then would agree to sacrifice years to the beast... only make me stronger, darker, so I might not fear any more

The abyss stared back; I became the darkness, a lie and a haunt until I feared no more but embraced death as I only understood willingness towards.

Why; the fear; it would dance around my bedroom when I was small, tormenting me, beckoning me to lose grasp upon the Rock, though I was small it succeeded to develop a weakness that would endure until my mind gathered a plot to end what was so dreadful, so lonely. I became surrounded with recklessness and began to build tolerance to substances that average men would fear, they would never know the power of an ally-

My person was now altered by my own hand, all that I wished for was now given to me in abundance by the power of a great delusion

I used and I used and I taught others to use, they adored me for I had what they sought after... a great knowledge of evil

I descended deeper than most of them, there was only one other with me that night that delivered me unto the rising sun for I did not escape, it scorched my skin, I grew thirsty, there was no relief, my ally showed its true self; a hideous dragon appeared amongst the smoke of the lower shaft, reaching for my heel to bruise, he came as I was weakened; no one to influence, no one to rule, it was I left in this blackened basement, my mind losing its perception of time; for it was night, then I was taken and the sun assaulted me, I felt dirty and hollow and wanted to be within the earth. The hours fell as stars from a shaken fig tree- black holes within the eclipsing reality of my life descended slowly before my eyes, about the size of grapefruits and they were pitch black, around them an ultra violet band, irregular, silver twinkle, thin, would orbit then vanish, this was life; its last burn against a horrid early death,,, the one whom I was with looked helplessly at me with eyes like a child; the child we all thought we had successfully left behind was now exposed once more to be helpless and dying, I was no father, only deceived, I could do nothing for him as he would turn away each time to vomit, I would sink back into my slow death and watch the pitch black emptiness of my deeds burn against what had become my life... a blackened basement, a silent flickering television set, a sun or a moon whose light failed to pierce the concrete walls of my consequence and a child, a bastard, whose fruit is vomit-

From those hours, a.m. and p.m. emerged two souls; I was slow and ponderous, the other went ahead to begin this new night for the last one had passed; I said you're going out? He answered yes.

I do not know how much was too much for I only knew to take it all, clean 'em out, steal, persuade, con, promise, flatter, whatever it took to get me on, all I knew was I was an army of tolerances and I would need enough to alter my person once more even after the mass would fall out; so to lead them to bliss as they watched with weary tired eyes the man, the beast, ride into the next oblivion-

Except this time it was different, I was not thrust onward, I was not proud of my tolerance, no, I believed rather that I was spared, spared from that death and that dragon and those holes in reality that were black, black... black as I was, yes I realized, realized I was the one, led astray as plunder, the plunder of my own soul- that dragon stood there waiting to devour my very heart as my body swayed in the current of eternal death, barely standing, no one kicked, no one shouted, GET UP GET UP YOU PUSSY. No, there was no one, nothing but the end of my flesh, its sentence and my teacher whom had delivered me to his own gloomy darkness, I was fooled and wounded, left and dying and still, I lived.

I do not remember what took place the next few days for as I said it was all like a dream, not just that night but the whole thing, the whole dance, it started with those first nights out, that allure, that freedom, our neighborhood, it started with my attitude, my lust, my greed, it started when I realized that I could recreate myself into a beast that would not fear but would be feared, it started with them, it started with us... I inherited a passion for knowledge, a knowledge that surely led to destruction though I believed it would only lead to power, no, power was given to keep me entangled and as each craft became mastered another would arrive right on time, I should have looked at the drivers face, funny I never thought to look, the car would just pull up, the passenger would signal to me and I would grab the magic, I thought I was a god, giving them their power, the car would leave and not show again until I was ready for something stronger, darker and closer to Sheol. Somewhere after that night I did realize my entire teenage life span was over and I wondered about that, I wondered; I counted the years on my hand and wondered, I thought of its beginnings in the park and wondered, I thought of its cars and fights and girls and wondered, I thought of its smells and spells and calls and wondered, its clothes and its trips and its travels and wondered, I wondered and wondered and wondered; of its nights and songs, its meetings, searches, rival feuds and bankings, monies spent, mornings in bed, days and days and days wasted, offered up and given for the simple rush of running around; no I knew there was more, I knew there was more than an adolescent joy ride that occurs in every generation- I was shown the play, the game, the rules and when I thought I was in charge I was shut down. No, I knew for certain what had happened so I chose.

"JOSHUA"; I heard my name spoken in thunderings, I was awakened and scared, Lord, Lord, sweat came over my body I moved from the room and searched my heart of hearts; God, PLEASE, what do I do- "You have been away living in this death, this allusion the beast served to your own appeal, you must forsake this ideal, you must believe in whom I have created and serve. Ascend from this shelter he has offered you, son of man you must prophesy to many people and nations and tongues, for this reason I have called to you and have saved you from your own doings, I have chosen you for greatness, in this you must believe, trust in me and the power of my Spirit for I will make your head hard as flint, I will make your head as hard as their heads and you will speak unto them and testify, your inner fire has been given to you- you will wage war against the beast who sought to devour you and you will be victorious in good warfare, do not fear them, be strong and courageous, do not be terrified, do not be discouraged, I the Lord your God will be with you wherever you go."

Therefore nothing can keep me from this for it is God who commands me- what can separate me from this love, can angel or demon, we then are more than conquerors who endure, more than conquerors who defeat him with the blood of the Lamb and our testimony, more than conquerors who remember the great height from which we fell before being ransomed by Him for Him. More than-More than any force, any knowledge, More Than any beast or dragon, any world or culture, more than any mark or tribulation, See He has made us more.

MORTALS SEE NOTHING

The wind smooths over the surface of the substance
Much like the hand that labors
This Ghost moves with a force like water
Static, Wave
Making straight the path of the Lord
Staring into the reflection there is no abyss
The Light
Almost disappearing
So white it is no longer there
Mortals see the invisible as nothing

OH THE IMMORTAL SENSATION

I was day dreaming of you
when the sound of dogs howling gave compliment to Godowsky
Oh the immortal sensation
I believe it to be, "faded blossoms"
Or another ultra romantic plea
without words to taint what is perfect
heaven darkened
Oh earth
And sea
woe, woe to thee
For the day of lovemaking did cease
twas bought and captured in fantasy
though the full number of gentile heard
there were many found asleep
If only one more night to watch
If only we'd become a falcon
wild and unafraid
He has come
this great and terrible day
in hidden hour
like a thief
like emptiness grasping a little child
while bathing in a tub of silence
Flowers no longer appear on the earth; the song left unsung
still all those moments alone I thought of you
Oh the immortal sensation
all those moments I thought of you
Oh immortal sensation

OBSESSIONS ARE FORFEITED WHEN REALIZED OR SACRIFICED

Requiring both the latter being the way to end the habitual practice
pink edge just slight where it meets her smallest blond hairs
fine and delicate up her spine even continuing into her mind- this
is a secret place
where what is realized is also translated to a plain gesture
her longest beat shortened flow decreased-continuum broken
confrontation evaded- thought spinning spunk
poured out- now a pervasive drink
reserved for a time suitable
consume it quickly before one could derive harm

A prudent man overlooks an offense
while a women defines each one by the last
still her prudence is seen
morning early tonight is too late
perfection loses to fate
I would be a good man but
we all would be great
if what we possessed was suddenly taken
there is the field- open and free
there you will enter the quietness far from all argument
trailing rainbows remain of the butterfly
with a promise not to harm in the pouring rain
away from there leading back a path torn through the edge of the field
we all went back one by one perhaps loneliness overcame
entrusting ourselves once again to a heart and a cage

NOTES

Sunken beat within her heart
Before Sebastian's masterful counterpoint
Cello- Harp, either or
All may claim; to be ashore
Of the sacred truth, of my sorrow, my love, my character to borrow
Who is to test with embargo
Of this war fighteth the lunatic
For favor of men and worthless jest
Quam operor notita teneo meus pectoris
One must eventually decline my truest Fabrizio, leave the garden of Cosimo Rucellai
Folly has clouded their minds from reason, envy begetting malice begetting high treason
Still the harmony of direst comforts, for he has placed in them His purpose
Without words I... reach and I... touch; a soul's glance; still more fulfilling then discourse
Handsome status relinquish thou thirst, for thy flesh permits thee sleep, though you were told to watch
I am weak and so I smile

WAITING FOR THE RAIN TO FALL

Waiting for the rain to fall
A memory to resurrect
A reason to believe or just plain accept
Sun will smile no ray today
Only gray is left
Wind doth whisper peace
Still the highway pilgrims wept
The train another sentiment or rather the rail its breath
A dream- a myth... THE WEST-
In the wilderness of flesh
Bread and wine are sacrament
Beauty haunts the committed soul
Forever unto death

SO OLD AT TWENTY SIX

BEAT the drum admit you have won praise to the sun of suns and declare it number one, again, again and again now you're done

Feel free to dance but hide your romance and believe it's worth your very soul to believe... AND BELIEVE IT'S WORTH YOUR VERY SOUL TO BELIEVE

Joy, joy, learn from the begging dog, learn from the prayerful bug and the shutter lens that blinks more in my hand then yours for I press and release your release, so stop kissing me for heaven's sake, for heaven's sake, for heaven's sake stop kissing me, goodness, sugar, good grief- sarcasm shakes hands with the superstitious religious, ethnic prohibits... all; that's not amended and the priest has left us for dead so jump out- jump in, your forgiven believe me it's worth your soul to believe me- the desert's been left for us to undress our skin besides the wolf- who let the darkness fall from the hand of that child she's grinning, your supposed to smile back, say hello, now goodbye, don't cry don't cry not now....-NOW...- NOW – now, believe me, believe me it's worth your soul to believe me and you have got to get your timing right, they will eat your conscience if you do not dress your best, don't worry about it are you excited bravo bravo, always state this twice, some things leave a bad taste like a threat unlike banana pie, you're my guy you're my cherry chocolates, you're my southern sky, you're my Spanish mistress, you're my night cap, you're my twilight kitty cat and the reason is... lost I can't find it, you're so great I just know it, besides this you're altogether ferocious now focus... how many twinkies am I holding up, let me show you to your seat you have been frozen in this photograph you must be exhausted I hope we can pick up right where we left off, now what did that contentious expression mean to relate, I miss you so much these days- oh those good old days- now you're gray and dull, it was always a pleasure to navigate around your cynicism, oh well what can I do. What can you do? Oh well. It is what it is, forget about it, no worries, you're old so old at twenty six-

PEACE

There is this brightness today, not from the sun per se- a hovering embodiment... kind of following me around but also going before me, as to start out into a room first through the door ahead- once I am inside I realize a most gentle radiance- within the atoms of the invisible air- life- pure substantial all filling life, even moving to the wide and open outdoors there is a sort of lantern before me... this very time of day- this very special presence of light- the glow we witnessed as children, widening the grasp upon reality... an elemental proof to our own existence, to our being, the personal touch of insight given to one's own self.

This peace, this quiet still peace- as if summoned by a spell of intrigue; searching for its essence in mankind, its importance for progress to take place- realizing "peace is the basis to progress"- as I am accompanied this day... this day before the first of September, I date myself spiritually knowing that this is a most grand stranger riding into a most lawless town- for my life has too long had its dwelling with him who hates peace. I am for peace; but when I speak, they are for war.

I was afraid of the knowledge bestowed to me- the findings of cruelty in the hearts of brethren- as if we all had adopted Cain; the world's hard forehead to beat against one another- to break one another- and so a lost art must be found... the art of kindness, for without it we are barbarians invading the cultures of each civilization we plunder... of each one's holiness, of each one's goodwill, the conscious of the mind of Christ- to misunderstand and to put thou under- not once seeing how beautiful this art form is- not once being instructed on how well it would go with us, we instead assumed the strong arm of human persuasion, the toughness and grit of business, as if it were an Egyptian man child with all the sophistication of a prominent empire; sent down along the rushes and reeds for the good of a nation- Therefore the peace had shown in an altogether other place... away from us... away from brothers. This is the peace prayed for Salem... this is the peace that begins all things anew- Light is formed - Darkness created.

LEOPARD

I am the shadow of the sun
The sun does not claim responsibility for me-
Only it lights a path when I am looking for trouble
Our dreams are harnessed by the hardened souls of America
For they are many
We who are few are also scattered
So we keep our insanity
Prophets, freaks and poets
The world is mad
We do not assume normality
For this would be a most intolerable contradiction
I am a leopard allergic to sulfur
From over the hill I will watch over the colony

MAY THE DAY IS MAY

I drank what was left in the glass
What it was I would have to ask
Took a static bath
Your voice like a crushing wave

I am on the shore of Sicily
Looking across for the goddess of Delphi
Always keeping an eye out for divine beauty
Quiet now I will swim to thee
The chant of irrational mortals is worry
So I cling to what you all would consider folly

Behind the commercial melody- screaming
Though distant I saw its sonic appearance

All of earthly perfection has an ever nearing eclipse of sorrow
For the prophets all agree that the days of darkness are many
Yet still remain the innumerable days of light

The machine that brought us here was formed by Saturn
Larger than the day star
The collection taken for the journey totaled over 177 thousand of
varied currency
For the ship held 202 ransom
They invested in the sky, the captain, the bird that flew them
through the clouds and the place
Held only in a dream before them before that day
We only saw the pictures of Ancient Beauty
We only knew the text
Today- Today
We breathe
Bunkers full of the working class refugee

Proletarians taking a bit of time for a tour
Me, I see everyone I have ever known in each one of their faces
Remaining is just a small mystery that only exists within departure
times, tickets and the relative you are with is relative- she can not be
tamed nor explained, how you met ways is God's secret unfolding in
the Divine Dance, a secret angel's giggle about- the immortals charted
our ancestors like stars until the present arrangement, the argument,
my fathers father's 107 father had with his Polish Princess-
She is a Queen

As for you my beautiful baby boy, my day passes quantum as you
sleep with moon rays shimmering on your newly given coat for
I have been brought to the rising of the Sun

Sat guru on a black beach of stone while listening to the ocean sing
in a different tone
Lower than the whisper when making love to the sand
Was offered all the spiritual widows; No, I stated- I am most
content under the shade of the sun
As I awoke it all just slipped away- there was nothing- I was no
one- and could only look forward
I was far away, not from home but from who I once was

Sparrow- I command you to come out
Yes; I wrote much of life- my life - our lives
The Albino Owl promised I would be most advantaged in
revealing the mystery of who I Am
And I must digest each little piece of the Christ as it is given to me
By the way Sparrow you are most dark by pointing out the obvious
truth and painting it black as you are- as if learning yourself- as if
learning anything could be as wrong as you suggest- Still Father
feeds you and is your kind sutler

There is a beautifully pleasing Russian Princess I once made
acquaintance with
At first I had thought she was the One traveling for her Czar in
search of the Greco lady bug with no spots but a black W painted
over its red shell by the unknown God of the Athenians-
She would place this in his empty chest and hope for her people a
heart would form-

Only she was not alone but with Prince- the Grossly Disfigured Prince of the Capitol World-

Controlling her with Ancient Supremacy a bushy black mustache proved

I felt a pain for her that did not require much imagination to conjure for it is a mutual inheritance the Divine bonds to us passionate ones- a permanent yoke-

Like the cracked earth bearing witness to its relationship with the Sun

We fortunate vessels crack at sea and witness our own sinking-

Always being reinvented by Him who resurrects us from many deaths

So to enjoy the next slaughter-

My soul has a number on it and so did hers- I feared she was nearing that number

She witnessed her own tragedy with each changing of the tide

As the ever churning Mediterranean mocked her beauty in its contradiction to her circumstance

What could she do besides endure her placement- he brought her away- she could not escape

For this already was intended as such

So to seem enchanted with the specific carvings of the Earth-

The Eternal Father so drug His finger through this land and through her heart forever

So to bear as a symbol of the hope we the Chosen have growing in us

As a pear tree to once litter the grass beneath for the lesser to feast upon our fallen fruits

For we let them go- we let them fall away from us and rot whether into the sacred ground or into the cursed gut of beasts and swine who devour even pearls-

Poor girl you say- you have not flown off yet sparrow, has not this place and truth troubled your false perception- has not your wing urged you to flight- to where men only speak of passing falsehood and meaningless affairs- Listen here: she is a piece of straw added to your nest, you carry her off in your beak to place her where you wish and she is there to stay amongst many others who are tangled and woven for the purpose of another creature-

For amongst ancient beauty one could be held captive by the most modern cruelty

Leave me now, fly to a place of blind seekers and let this ax be at the root-

Or perhaps I should be silent- I would tell Angel to never interrupt
a content moment
Let that be charged to someone else's account
So sit then and listen as a Spy, as a false inquisitor-
the more iniquity stored in the silo of your coming judgment

With many strikes I finally succeeded to separate the pain from the
kindly given gift
Even in the metaphysical state it appeared as a stone- really a
hardened nut from the jungles of Quito
I always adorned its color even when it was handed over to me by
the embittered jealous steward
Since then I tried to divide the gift from the hatred
844 days and now in this moment you of all fowl witness this faded
teal dolphin come off
See the chipped surface proving my attempts
Now before thee I cast the dolphin into the unfamiliar sea- as to say:
I hated the yeast that was added for a time,
it leavened the bread yet still I let it hang with the other gems
So into the tide fair well Keen Serpent swim away
Swim far away or die against the black rock

Oh yes forgive me if I do not allow you to speak
For it is bad enough I have to hear all those you have deceived
What's this now you claim; a good tiding- oh go on-
I could not muzzle you for so long a time to deliver mankind
A story- I shall be attentive- a time piece, yes go on-
A time piece that afforded time to its keeper
Delivered by a passing logic that suited this brawn Son of Cain-
Passing through many lands it was laid upon him by many
maidens to remain free of question
He cared not for permanent meaning relevant to his true self but
adjusted to many traditions
Though you would consider this child lost he continued to find beauty
Those he met did not think to commit him as they closed the town gate
At any sign of vexation he quickly would depart

What than will you strain to convince me- this man found his
heart's true state by turning from aggression, and... so where is
your trick, what guise does this serve for- perhaps you should ask

how this quest began, every man has a soul – every Child's birth a
Star – a being to their conscience – your man has no existence, not
as a peaceful sage
We all must decide what is noble to leave behind and worthy to
tend- or even buy from the Merchant
Ah yes if you have exhausted all your breath may I suggest that I
am the Merchant-

Days pass without us telling them so
As we place the parts of living to tip the scale-
Unable to afford the consequence of the weight measured to one side-
I always come up short reaching deeper, smiling at the eternal
merchant as if he cares of my passing-
What is the cost of a balanced scale
"I do not know"
What is the point of a balanced scale sir-
I can tell you
To prepare.
I am the merchant and the buyer-I sell and I buy to and from myself

What are you grinning at- So do you-
What to leave and what to pick up, time continues mocking-
Serenading us when we are alone to seek others, pushing us on our
way soon enough to be- just to be-

There is no possession that has the power to satisfy- nothing is as
powerful as the dream
The dream allowing us to accept the idea
This means all envy is foolishness for it is not as great as that which
takes focus in the mind-
The man you speak of follows a thought with the expectation of it
manifesting into a better reality
Appearing out of thin air just for being sought after
We destroy in order to create and all of civilization approves
In search of something better we allow the wolf and vulture to
devour what we would not preserve
A dream is for the mind- all that the Father gives is Life
To live Life is to thank the Father of Lights
Stillness – peace – I have been born over
From here I can now say even all this is not the total proof

For I speak to a full Moon and even tomorrow the angle will deplete
So sleep
Beneath you the ever rotating truth
Above the mirror of reflection
Even if the clouds may hinder
The Holy Wind carries clear redeemable views-

SCALE

Hello child of God,
Yes it has been so, so crazy around here,
I actually took off today to tell Jehovah I want him to have it all back-
I walked through the forest and said amen and amend-
I am seeing life as if it were a scale; I am just not sure how just its
sums are,
You should come by anyway, just come by to say hello-
Days pass without us telling them so
As we place the parts of living to tip the scale-
Unable to afford the consequence of the weight measured to one side-
I always come up short reaching deeper, smiling at the eternal
merchant as if he cares of my passing-
What to leave and what to pick up, time continues mocking-
Serenading us when we are alone to seek others pushing us on our
way soon enough to be- just to be-

I CAME AN HONEST MAN

I asked my friend to leave
He said you know I can't leave
I told my friend I would miss him
He replied; because I stay you know where I will be
My friend, my friend the woods
I than will go and you will stay here-

Hinge it upon me I asked once, hinge it upon me I asked again
Looking up at passing clouds with borrowed spectacles
My peripheral entangled with flags flickering from lampposts
Like flames influenced by the wind
Refusing to walk down the ally of familiarity
I will wait till the next street the next city if need be-

I came an honest man I left a thief
Hawk peers down with laser sight awaiting the expiration of life

The hawk is black but has a white wisdom that witnesses
The hawk sees
how the cowboy grazes

The hawk sees
when the wheat heads are softly lit by the morning star
The hawk sees
the reflection of Eden shining from the soul of man in the warmth
of spring

The hawk sees
us stop and consider the silence of our mortality as the leaves let go
of the limbs they suckled

The hawk sees

how the cowboy tilts his hat against the northern trade wind sent
by Ull to disperse all fantasy

The hawk sees
all that is below him- in this way he gains knowledge

Children seek the albino owl between the eves of abandoned barns-
for his inherited truth
Along the sides of timeless fields highway ghosts travel
Placing horrific tales of life to death onto the tongues of transit men
Becoming a present myth, achieving reverence in the oral retelling
The boy commanded his vulcanized horse to an innumerable speed
through a toll without paying Charon, bypassing the river and
entering the everlasting realm as a flash of light- his thrill destined
to be sealed by himself only- seeing fate wave him through- he felt
the wings of invincibility-
The song, was too low for him to hear, what I heard was her voice-
The essence of an adolescent fantasy-

STRUGGLE OF LOVE

I can feel the warmth of the one who sat here before me
should I wonder- it could have been you
should I race- should I allow the wind over my shoulder blades
were Adam and Eve Chinese
they certainly weren't eating American cheese
I would like to know of the Islamic woman's golden tattoos
circling and intersecting on the surface of her flesh
what do they mean
they advise me by saying- you should be happy not all lovers love
so completely
distracted by Orientals – bet they're great at studying
dog tired at the wheel- she wants your love
falling asleep, two eyes closed and one opened- I heard Angel singing
demons kept quiet as they reconsidered their permanent decision
the albino owl flew past me- and dissolved into the crescent of the
moon
the chant continued as I became unaware-
with gentle whispers they declare-

Bring us closer to the crest Lord Jesus
Bring us closer to the Crest of Zion
HIGHER and HIGHER
Bring us higher to the crest

On the wings of honor
we follow Apostles and Prophets in love truth and kindness
bring us higher
bring us closer to the crest LORD J E S U S
And send therefore to Joppa-

After this I was no more and rested from the struggle of love-

THE MEXICAN MAN

The Mexican man of the winter lakes, the winter lakes filled with the cold sensation of rain which falls from the clouds that hover around the crest of Zion, once seen one begins to wonder- who is this man- he winks, he yawns, he peers throughout the room awkwardly only to realize the seat that is open is right before him- he sits and looks intently at a small hard to handle book with a ridiculous sales tag stuck to the binding- you look away, then back- and he's gone- having every right to wander, look and stare at the beautiful women and men; for I ponder and direct my attention to him- how can we go on like this- how can we continue down this broken road together, lacking zealous intrigue- I only know a few good professors to quote "madness as a form of health" the rest seem rotten with pride. I will escape with the hymnals of Barber's Adagio- alive within this unspoken grace: the heart of hearts hidden to keep melancholy safe- I don't see the world changing for me, the clock shows less the eclipsing hour; so much has past we are swallowed in ignorance due simply to the magnitude of all that was before- sheering courage for intellect, promoting cowards to stay at home- it's raining out and grief is sorrow and so is knowledge- why ignore what you know to convince me of the obvious-

Ramp of Pharaoh pierces pyramid capstone, descending galaxy though I'm reaching quantum leap, which will arrive first I do not know, not the greatest just becoming least- want to change the whole program- I hate the program- Get real or get lost...

HURRY

Hurry up before we lose our place in society
LETS GO, you'll lose my place in His story
Keep your voice down before I forget my fate
I was going to help you before I was commanded to do so
The son that changed his mind was the one deemed valiant
You seem to forget I Am the prodigal questioning the establishment
THAT WON'T SHUT ITS MOUTH EVEN TO SAVE ITSELF-
Expensive furnishings inspire women to lay in the nude securing
their place in luxury
Pardon me I should have looked away when the voluptuous truth
appeared before me
How do I define my obsession- perhaps simpler than I make it and
still too complicated for you
We all know beauty when we see it- its attraction is universal-
within a frame a face and form- an image, an image... of God

PARIS PHOTOGRAPH

She is presently beautiful
as Angel once was
the world has aged Angel most unkindly
perhaps it was my mind to say more wisely

the eye is never full
and what it sees it judges harshly
still it is most partial to mystery, cruel to what has become
disclosed

my lips and tongue could be still for a year's time
if only that fox would stop laughing by the permission of twilight
if only I could live with the river tribes- Arizona priest and
Montana sky
see the true story is complicated with lies-

this is a money market
we shop here- nice to make your acquaintance
our women dress in fortune cookie shells

it is all meant to be taken lightly
let me go become myself
to own the landscape Emerson promised me
they will do sophisticated tests on the skin left by the river Jordan

Lao Tzu shares calmness saying- "nature does not hurry yet
everything is accomplished"
I can not find a place to sit or stand whether in the pew or on stage
I will be waiting by the back door- until you all achieve the
morning rituals
ceremonial succession to which I am a combatant

I have seen enough stunning women to die an unsatisfied man
the autumn foliage like fruity pebbles
I am a very rich prince lost in my father's jewels

the times have always beckoned
trying to crush the spirit of man
the impression of jealous revenge

one driven harder faster by the other- and for what
to crack a nut- to bring greed to glory- vainglory
depart to the forest- construct forts and traps, wait with drawn bows- let them burn the last village and consider sawing the last timber- be sure they will for their spirits are destined to drink of the dregs- objects of wrath- God said it best- some mass is required for shape and trance needed for vision- so do not lock all the doors; open when persistence wakes you up at night even when your children are asleep in their beds and please do not mistake my words with the one who quietly climbs in over the wall- the thief be caught- while mercy peace and love walk freely.
Approaching boredom need a place to photograph
think I'll take a scooter to Paris France

EZRA

"At the evening sacrifice I arose from my depression" this was uttered from the mouth of brother Ezra and it's all that- see the stoic men of the decade would afford the time to convince you that the experience of sadness is an unnecessary evil for unbelievers- please brothers, sisters take to heart what I reveal to you and learn for yourselves the spiritual language, become acquainted with the character of God- His reactions to the ways of man are written out-

His chosen men have behaviors toward trial and understanding toward mercy- we have our way and philosophy repeated- hundreds of personalities perceiving a Christ like perspective- do not admit some doctrinal decree- become a patron saint amongst the living- the reasons for sadness differ, strive in your compassion to weep in the love and Spirit of the Messiah

LESBIAN

They think they're lesbians but really they're alone and if they even knew that pretending for a moment could cause the heart to harden even harder than stone such things are possible- we think it so sexy that even the senses are helpless as they deaden if you could hear your soul darken- you would wonder why- why did I attach myself to a theory expecting fact to transpire and now that your eyes have met his you will make a sudden change, good thing the world has names names to pardon their false explanations- so let me tell you what I think unashamedly- you are just crazed full of fantasy- and so am I child it's fine- only admit it's never as good as it would seem- sensitivity of flesh but it only produces fruit towards a temporal touch and so ripened on the vine it rots

ENOUGH SHOULD BE ENOUGH

Human conquest seems to be filling the air we breathe- not only on the corporate level individuals around me are closing in can I decide to put distance between us- build a cabin and spend the day chopping wood to warm it a pleasure to myself- we exchange time for currency and currency for stuffing- when does it end how professional must I be- are the days of cowboys and travelers so far off that evangelists must enlist with a church's organization and powers that be what is free when even our thoughts are focused on industry- may I have my mind back my heart is becoming lonely crying to a beat of melancholy- will it return soon at least for the full moon we have all grown up to be such responsible adults doing exactly what the world has taught us

CROWS

Field of crows, one tied to another

one sound and many pairs of wings lift to defeat gravity

the scare crow overthrown, the shadow eaten

the ground itself blackened

oil rainbow

who in the depth of night spots a crow

Sir Hitchcock cape

as I work they look down from the tree tops-

the crows all laugh at me

a gang,

a mob in black trench standing on the green and blue country side

TODAY

Today I was sick, really it's been a few days and I'm not sure if I can cope
Losing sight of the destination- maybe it's my sanity I have sacrificed
I always thought it was my freedom- the world's handling it just fine
ya right- the world keeps borrowing from itself-
Like it could go on forever like traffic on the highway
Makes a man not mind dying, makes him wanna stop tryin'

Father is it not the hour to put a stop to their operation

AS ONE

And we will be as one
Understanding each other
Feeling each other
Truly knowing each other
In love with each other
Then there will be Harmony

SO THIS IS IT

So this is it I'm going to die
the sum of my life's breath
speaking to me like a child taking me for one last ride
to hear the sirens rise

so this is death never mind the reasons why
peaceful this morning for a change I should just lay here

do not be afraid you'll be fine sure - it's just the sirens so loudly
crying
was peaceful until now my death seems their panic
those days until now all have been a terrible trial
scared everyday of my own child
as the sun sets regrets start knocking on the door- circling my house
peering through the windows seeing I am alone

today I have forgotten and letting go I draw nearer as the reverent
try to intercede
but I am fine really I fell asleep in the most peaceful state
it was there I was assured and felt complete
I seemed to have lost my most cherished fear
must have slipped from my hand- or heart I'm not quite sure
shaking- who IS shaking ME! I was awakened with the concern for
my temple
speaking to me as if I were just born, the faithful passing me off to
the professionals
the door that is not used for passage opened, light poured in searing
my eyes
now strangers take the place of my reverent guides
piano music awkwardly continued as my life passed- back- from
the hand of God to man

THE TREE

The tree had no fruit only leaves and yet even its life was taken
which way do I go to get back to the flesh
only then will I be worthy to be trampled on by men
this plow hurts let me remove my hand to rest
Jesus in the wilderness with the most seductive wolf
whistling down a dusty path
the devil tempted but the spirit led
the wolf follows me all the way home and chooses to appear once I
am asleep
mother- father- teacher- brother- friend-
loving them all more than the Son proves to be abusive
I wish to be a sort of vessel, a cloud blown by the wind
led along for outpouring
there the Spirit brings me to give what I truly received
droplets of guilt and sorrow drizzle down my melancholy
countenance
do not pity or squirm
I hold within my soul's eye a single moment
like those who strive to see an elemental column
I tune in to the frequency in my head- around my heart and
through the pulse of others
here I am a scientist of wonder
variables coming together for me to perceive
divine perspective; sovereignty

ROMANCE

Romance is lust's first expression
dress it up as you will
commitment being as sheer boredom
I should have warned you of me-
allow me to utter a big fat SORRY
I am pathetic- elastic will
just let me breathe
all guilt trips arrive Here
destination little white pill
serotonin drenches my receiver
leaving a soul to finance a great depression
God create me again-
I have been born of water and ghost
still I can not relate to this relationship
the end of a story, the way he looked, as he walked away
if not for the fashion of his day and his cloak being a bright blue sky
how stoic he would have seemed
I resented his wall street aggression
the wall will burn without a dime of mine, soldered with no tear
vehicles lend me to a southern breeze
I would like a dangerous place please-
America for the handicapped and over privileged
his sideburns intersected with his mustache
looked real twill, you know what I mean
mother and daughter expressed sparkling admiration over fresh
brewed coffee
and the homosexual walked back and forth several times perfecting
his stride-
passing from intrinsic to unnatural
see how image corresponds with personality
clashing or accommodating

the small china man with the toothpick between his shriveled lips-
his entire head measuring five inches from chin to calic
people get old, people are born- bees buzz to hear the sound they make
vanity, vanity sings the king
Harvard grad meets subway refugee passing to pass through the
bowels of a city
a city shows the true intent of man- his delusion- lust and greed-
the material passion to keep moving away from the unsightly and
closer to the overwhelming appeal
moths corrupt uncounted generations of tradition along with the
current expectation simply because they eat fabrics- we are the
epitome of what we accuse others
a smell can be more terrifying than a site
the fellow with the drums is leaving already, the kids must have
booed him out
the difference between then and now- I compare everything
at this place I can see the only hill in the land
Contented heart drifts to feel life pass under him
unsatisfied soul wanders to digest lives and defecate on others- we
defecate our unhappiness on those closest- we defecate our egos on
the best of friends- stuffing ourselves into their ears
as long as it's tucked in with buttons on it they will be happy-

FAIRS WHEEL

I am in a deficit
I am a deficit
up and down all is moving onward- upward- downward
circulating through my mind

around and around
fairs wheel will not let me off
around and around- trivial notes sound off
around and around
children running dizzying themselves, running around looking up at
me
as I go around and around and around and around
something has gotten in unlock the doors let me out
am I the only one that can hear me scream
Father can you hear me screaming
do you scream- Jesus do you still weep; is it because of me
so what happens if I have lost this winning streak
was it even or just a hippie idealistic belief

I hate my every breathed opinion
bury every prideful mindset beneath
I would much rather be a lover of the wild terrains of the earth
to think of spending my days censuring all that culture births

entangle me in morning walks through forests where no one talks
listening to the birds and swaying trees, the still frames of lakes and
chanting rivers
all of their expressions bred with pure intent-
having to understand man's plot for conquest- observing the
motives of tradition-
ALL that's in the minds landscape of unholy man

for in the circle of madmen I rest
in the circle of madness we are all run down- where is the albino
owl to fly me away
the earth has been waiting for me, truly waiting, it has been all along

when will I be released from societies turn
a chance to freely learn
consumerism ate the souls of those shopping
even then they sang tis a vi
money must be paid, slave to the lender

youth betrayed the future's peace
death is peace, death is release, killed myself before
seems numbers and figures are indestructible
they knock persistently- seeking to receive- owing my master
diligence till death do us part
the modern credit companion
and what do you want from me Father- simply everything

GHOST

What was that sound
was it the wind, a holy ghost

The Holy Ghost
Is it only children
fearful of spirits
who's walking on the water
is it a ghost A Holy Ghost
When I was a child
still much a child
what was that sound, who's walking on the water
calming the winds
waves obeying Him
is it a ghost, a son of man

WHY WE MARRY

Why do we marry why not live alone with occasional company allowing our personalities to grow independently until evolving into their uninterrupted perfect [whole and complete] selves - why choose one to cling to cry and wake beside - why marry why sacrifice our very oneness - some marry for wealth and others to obtain various fantasies shaped by the illusions of a spiritually bankrupt civilization leaving spouses with only themselves with no practical wisdom promoting togetherness instead a drifting dream of a very aesthetic lifestyle vanishing before there hardships - why do we marry it becomes a different reason with every lesson learned - marriage is an opportunity a vow to not give up on just one person while we pass through the years of this our given life - to love just one to bend to one to find rhythm to gain strength to defy selfish desire to relent in complaint grasping tenderness losing grip of self and becoming love - becoming love -this is the greatest of qualities and can overcome all darkness - one who must defeat hate a test to defeat all sorts of evil within yet has been given to marriage has their way - to love is to find truth and the warmest of truths love one another and become healed made warm - the leaves are changing may this season of our hearts color bleed a deeper red may God bless you both my beautiful mother and father I truly seek to love you both deeper each day.

EQUALLY AS MUCH

True I love to go into the city
I love to leave equally as much

coming and going to and from the city
but for some there is no time to go

keeping within the city limits- entranced in commerce
just as those who came on boats- before them- no one remembers
they all forget- hoping for better years for it all ends one ordinary day

modern man is found staring deep into your photograph
random book
random thought
random man but now you're gone
your eyes replaced by his

restless sin is a city
with all its avenues
as a castle her square
containing culture- fellowship of pleasures
village sage and saxophone players
the city is always there- welcoming anyone with her calloused eye
those who were once rejected appreciate the cold embrace of her
indifference
the liberty of being no one
better a shadow on the great wall of a city
than to be known in a stuffy small town

TWENTIETH CENTURY MATTER

Arrived the whole
twentieth century matter
boatman cried aloud
I have not the muscle for a crowd
besides too horrible a hell for flames
how did this all become
I mean me asking these

something adrift
seems an urchin
to move me from Styx
come, come move along
who are thou to know this song
centuries past did not foresee
leave the coins beside the tree
I hummed swayed and proudly stood
the urchin lost on a substance trip
beside the dragon i have not a fear
with all that guilt
who would not tempt me to steer clear
still there is time
to strengthen the shell of this ride

world still lost
revolutionaries crying
any more there is no agreement
for a cause worth fighting
kill the prophets
rally still for revelry
revolution too high a cost for dying

STREAMING

Life is slow at times like a stream massaging every stone as it rolls over- evoking every grass blade to bend with a mutual intention to please- for the times of passive movements are many and alike and so awaiting a torrent is a guilty desire hidden in the heart of the stream and bed- the flood is only the wake of this happening after the complete measure of absorption has been reached- an excess of substance is a crushing weight over the foundations of necessity now covered in sweet intent, one would need to search for the catalyst pushed deeply to the bottom of the civilization- In the time of the swift running current only glimpses of detail show through and mimic the sensation- the sensation- a charge- life living and choosing for you, those moments demanding balance, composure, mental agility- for the sake of gracefully complimenting the thrill of the cosmic dance- passing through the breast of divinity nourishing the warrior child to discern while moving at the speed of light, hearing the music as it were when it played more than a millennium ago-

Able to imagine the times to come on mountain pass, prophets again with staffs, leading herds through the tribulation- the admiration of rudimentary skill given back to the natives like the transfer of taste through the nasal passage-

WITHIN THE WOODS

Within the woods lay a book unread by men however riddled by a bug with a strong sexual appetite his friends call him – insex preferring a certain sensuality formed by words consuming parts of cognitive thought leaving the filler that excuses the work art maintaining the liberty of being neither wrong nor right entrusted between the covers are flashes of nudity creating literal tension while seeking opportunity the essence of invisible matter highly congratulated when eloquently captured even the darkest part of night is kept lit when our passion sets ablaze our bodies grasping the once child now man armed with a vocabulary to tap into the mystery of compulsion the creative power of the word differing between flesh and spirit, the difference between life and death, strength and bondage, faithfulness and infidelity choosing hastily due to the curse we have eaten doomed to waste away as a result of foolishness cherished swallowing it whole sending it deep into our pit, into the center of our very being, captured by what we captured, turned on by our other self, deceived by vanity as deep as oblivion, our vanity a dark pool in which there is no reflection only a seductive draw

ONE OF THE LAST DAYS OF SEPTEMBER

I sat on a neglected, broken down porch
looking out to a field with only the sky to cover it
tractor trailer stampede stillness now recovered
the hypnotic chant of creatures too minute to see
send their call upwards against grass blades
knowing well their effect on man interrupting the confidence held
in human reason

there certainly is a freedom to the fields
yet with undertones of loneliness it stands as a poetic drama
could its solace beauty only be meant for a passing gaze
the breeze rolls over my thoughts
I am intoxicated with a place in time
slight chill reminds- one of the last days of September but please do
not bother me with the exact date

classic impala rusts into clay the days of its glory are no more
no more are the tires ripping into stone and no more is the affection
the driver had for the car

at last I stood very still
I noticed how a fence harnessed a perspective
large timber held an industrial lamp and to its right a bedroom
window
who... has stayed in that upper room
as steward to the gazing of the field

I move on
accept the truth of how small I am
hidden like the creatures in tall grass

there are countless places held still
how they stir life restless
agitated by passions
limited to a mortal being

1:53AM

Fantasy plagues my mind as if I were a child, only accompanied with the horrors and grief of mature knowledge- God save me from the coldest of truth from the cruelest hand of humanity for the mind is oh so fragile and it hurts so, for days it has hurt make it stop- forgive me Father for my thoughts are piercing- to what state must I return or to which way must I progress- Abba I only feel the awful sting of death and all it encompasses, there now must be another threshold to lend my devotion, my utmost attention- from here I only know and what I know the mind can not absorb to sustain me I will break if not led by the ghost it must bear this burden for I am sure the mind will snap I have in past reached this point of sensitivity there soon must be a transfer, restless without sleep and You know the ignorant will only mock and suspect evil- do not let shame fall upon your seer- for what task have You given me this sight and now the precepts of holiness I hold dear they guard me for I am an agent of Life thus an enemy of those dying- feed my soul courage in this hour for I am filled with the sorrow of much knowledge Where is the PURPOSE OF MY SALVATION- what is to become of this age and what am I- and what of them- for where will their perceptions fall into their children's hands into their enemies: into the misguided good intended- should I now in the midst of the darkest dynasty doubt that You are God that You are my Shepard that You love after me should I now in the pit of impotence decide to fold- to surrender- to give up the character I have seen You burn in trials of white flame and still it burns for Your sake that we might all be in You- for You- like You- should I now doubt my eyes and call them fatigued and disillusioned

WHAT DO I DO NOW- YOU TELL ME- GIVE YOUR COMMAND- I want deaf ears to the partial pleas of ambition the cries of fear dressed as mercy, make straight thy paths- for friends are like many divided rivers- can I watch over them without my flesh having proximity- guide my spirit to its seat even here amongst the living, show thee thy perimeters of dominion- for what has the training rendered besides a broken heart- my will is weakened by the day as the wind blows colder my heart beats less with vigor but still you can restore me like an eagle in high flight on the currents of the most terrible storm, all is well in the midst of struggle all is well in the carnal death the Victor has sealed the fate of fate and taken death hostage for the granting of life everlasting-

The wolves are roaming therefore we must know to what nature our engagement implies_ overtake evil by doing good & defeat darkness by exposing it to the light evil prevails by its deceit, cast out the mocker and the strife will end-

The lines have been crossed who will declare mutiny and to whom will be judged as traitor.

PERCEPTUAL PRECEPTS

DISCERNING THE DAY
PRELUDE.

Mind avenue
roll a nickel down the throat of the meter to park your shark
take a moment Please A moment
now absorb the sun china under you son......... listen with a rhythm
act like you can feel it
maybe you'll catch it though it's not a regular occurrence Never
mind -never mind that I smell like smoke

Why bother getting upset
See Mary, Martha learn from her

just what do you think the Scriptures are for
Sun lights the day so fear to be unconscious tonight
singing lullaby to you my dear listen ....
DON'T Envy and hide what you want
I have it right here
grasp the grapes, eat- you're seeing me enjoy
even before the foxes leave-

Bless him Eternal Father
bless the man - You show me truth and I love You for that, my
soul thanks you with endless thanks and praise- now for man; how
entrusted we are and thank you, thank you for the heart of flesh
and not of stone thank you, thank you God- You show me my
brother's hurts, the slashes of fiery trial accusation and assault from
mouthpieces of satanic chorus singing indoctrinated versus, these
that I do not even know you have placed in my path, they cry
before me even in public places thank you oh God thank you- our
helpers have lost their sight that gives faith and trust to the unseen,
these widowers of faith - for what is Yours that we don't receive- as

men we behold and enjoy it, thank you God, Yahweh thank you- even those I don't know closely and still you place them for me to look upon, they meet with their own brethren- confidants- friend closer than brother for them we thank you God, thank you – fellowship separated only by Holy Bible on table- Holy Confessions wife at home sharing zealously the contempt that holds him, He asks why? what more can I do ....can I give? For I have given her my very self- she just isn't happy, just isn't content I work all hours and still serpents breath, do I need stay on the corner of the roof or in the wilderness rather the accuser shouting for more security, So here I sob on your shoulder brother in this cloud surrounded even by pagan witnesses BUT I NEED RELEASE why doesn't she POSSESS PEACE, why all worry, why the worldly need when Father claims all responsibility- we are not orphans but royalty – still she pleads- a family has NEED NEED NEEDS monies insurances mans policies- man can not even lead in praise without his heart being wrought by the yoke of his spiritually sick equivalent, LeAVE leave now start to scream......

Sarah keeps laughing at Abraham's dream....

WHY, why CANT YOU JUST TRUST THE FATHER IN ME.

For all the men Satan is now trying to shake free from the Holy commitment in Christ, in the leaning of our entire personality on God, aware of the assault I stand firm for you in Spirit armed with Sword and rebuke against our adversary the Devil, The Lord rebuke you.

WARRIOR CHILD

I woke twice this morning
I woke once and felt nothing
I fell I fell back to sleep
And this is what I dreamed

Inside of someone's home on a refrigerator I looked at a picture
Of a man very mean with a scary story
my next perspective was walking behind this man
Looking at his bare back covered with tattoo and muscle
He was angry very angry and at me it suddenly seemed
He was spouting off threats one after another twisting side to side
like a provoked prize fighter
motorcycle helmet in hand he now walked past a vehicle I was now in-
aiming slurs and hurling tension on me
towards his bike he marched still threatening-
deep in my soul I heard a warrior child soon to be king calling back
rebuke to an unclean philistine-
whoever I was with in the car started to pull away-
the mysterious villain would follow behind -
just then a car approached from ahead blocking us to a stop-
his threats heard clearly continued on
and here is the strangest part of the vision at dawn- as the cars
stopped I walked up to my very self opened the door and looked
into my own pair of eyes stared deeply at myself looking back- I
saw myself at a young age of merely thirteen seeing much fear
contrasting an effort to be a man – a man of the world- I pulled and
tor at myself, pulling at my younger self while saying- *face him now
do not put it off, come on do it now.-*
And at that the dream was over-
Leaving me with a fascination the day would have to compete with
for my attention.

THE NEW JERU-SALEM

And I seen it all before
I seen it come
I seen it go away
But in this moment I have lost the will to ask you why
Exhausted I come to trust you blind
Maker of my days
Maker of each star
Fields blooming far away
Show me where you are
For certain reasons I can not see
You are building a place for me
In the third celestial sky
There's a project underway
To surprise all who thought they knew
Where eternally they would stay
A city for earth's new landscape
A place where His light will shine
And only the howling of the dogs will escape
Outside that great city's gate
Oh that place filled with grace
The grace of every generation
From the one the true God of Abraham of Isaac
And Jacob
The God of the living not the dead
That city filled with light
Crystal waters
Feeding the tree of life
The majestic stream
Pouring from the majestic King
Within those walls lives on lives on
That eternal kingdom

The New Jeru-Salem The New Jeru-Salem The New Jeru-Salem
The New Jeru-Salem

JONAH ANGRY

You can't go by what people say, Saint Millay
There is secret admiration where you think it least
Jealousy lurks like a drunkard in the shadow of weekend streets
Clumsy... ignorant... indignant
Still the reverent are silent
Watching and adding
As quiet as God
As eminent as Ming
As focused as a corporate neck tie
As willing as a city united together as one man
As wise as the wisest whom states "Open for me, my sister, my love, My dove, my perfect one"-
As full of blinding Love as He who obediently stretched out His arms to embrace death
As colorful as a rainbow prism, emerald, sapphire, onyx, Keith Green says like windows; stained
As underground iconic as an Ezra Pound mug shot
As I was saying, there are those who are trying to make up their minds About those who have
Who is who
Jonah angry; God asked: "is it right for you to be angry"?
As the plant withers the east wind blows... but the worm has eaten
The Lord giveth, the Lord taketh, the Lord giveth to someone else

THE SONS SUN

The dog barked on
After the sun
The sun could not turn back
As the dog had told
Only to pass
The people and plants
Throughout the world it rolled
Beaming continuously in defiance to
The thoughts of old
Silent blaring of fire
In the depth of space
Incomprehensible dark recess
Travel its ray
Imagine people waking to pain
As others dream impossible pleasures
Toiling and sweating both hearts beating
In the horizon of dusk and promised dawn
I foresee the arising of the fall from
Dividing light
The Son of Man arriving
Bringing every nation under day
Encircled by the sight of all people
Shining and outshining
The once gold medallion
Hung before the black silk
Of man's unanticipated end of reign
The beacon outdone by the creator of the sun -

TRIAL

A life ended before its intended purpose
The saddest feeling one could sense
Although a dream I faced my own death
Waking up downcast strongly affected by the affair
Ponderous morning brought on by subconscious despair
See the truth to every side, captured –saved all for perspectives sake
Sorting through the pieces of people in the world's puzzle game
Life is my teacher student of giftings
Trial and strife
My knowledge is limited to what I seek
For it to increase on with the weighted belt
And into the deep
Elders to their dismay
Dismiss what does not fit to the tradition of their day
Seeking vision from the prophet while the law perishes from the council
Wisdom bestowed to old age
Although blindly betrayed by yesteryear's routine
Confused as to what name should be given for an assembly
Gathered apart from a new moon
Tell me what is constructive on the sun's day
Once a week we meet
Yet unfulfilled the letter
Practicing song
Digesting the same professor's lecture
Drinking from the well of human effort
Lapping from a stream whose source seems lost
Power entrusted to the saints that have gone before us - gone into legend
So declares the prodigal
What of interpreting divine signals

Who is edified by the still tongue?
What sinner repents due to the prophet's regret?
A mystery unrevealed
A people strung in a system
God does not belong in your pretension to submission
Write your decrees fluorescent your flyer
With supernatural energy Jesus was shown as the Risen One True Son
Here your prayer only a pretext for a sign to claim
Realize the Way has long been underway-

OLD FRIENDS

Old friends are more like ghosts in my dreams
Senior Simon stated wisely I won't be convicted if by jury of my peers
And I simply agree
Past littered with moments belonging to those who have long been
dispersed
Could one fully know me only the eternal have seen
All the atoms within my mass those even that started with seed
What escaped is perpetually chasing
Melchizedek witnessed the whole
Accepted my tenth sent me away blessed
Although my ways were murderous and adulterous
Encouraging gluttony and rage
A priest forever pardoned
A limited life
An indestructible being
Preserved this mortal shell
For loss is gain
When He speaks I hear unrivaled wisdom so great not a man has
matched
I owe Him all just for giving me an ear to hear
Hebrew text expressed the nations regret; I freed you to serve only me
Man considers how to go on worthy of His King imitating
greatness that went before him
Those who traveled the dusty past of slavery
But still displaying the fruits of the Ghost
Doing as they did puts us on the wings of honor

BACK HERE

So I'm back here, back where you put me
Who can struggle against the hand of God
I can do so many things but going upstream tires me so – it – tires me so
Enthroned upon His Holy Mount
You must excuse all other paths to this state
Climb to reach Him stretching your limbs through elevation
Buzzard's wing grazes your neck looking to the crest blinded by the rising star
Seeing my very faith tied to my soul anchored to hope only a messiah can withhold
Perpendicular to the cord my lust and rage advertise on the horizon of my will
Seeing more vivid with my mind's eye
Yet embrace laid cold hand seldom even reaching towards Babylon's guise
As temptress she provokes the senses of man
Summoning devils to wager
Commander of God's army has knighted me with sword
So for the outside world I possess self control
For from the tree of the knowledge of good and evil
Bear forth spiritual fruit
Choosing to be Holy the will has no choice but to fight violently
Still revival pours as pure water from the pinnacle of life
Even washing away those who are unstable Intrigue gripped my understanding as He uttered direction

A PERSPECTIVE UNDER THE JAMAICAN SUN

There are many answers hidden within words, many questions to be
confronted in other worlds
most of which are often overlooked- much of man's eye confined to his own
mind

Doesn't take long to become where you are-

It was the fifth day maybe the fourth I don't know, whatever the correct count that day I woke feeling not a guest but at home – at home within myself that is- I had stopped seeing that which was right before me and returned to my normal state of viewing- seeing further out the beauty that surrounds me seeing the big picture - relaxed- not tense my face comfortable, my skin naturally adhering to its muscles as my current age allows, as I feel completely free to take time for granted not pressed but being pressed only by the breeze I sit to write and to eat my twelfth helping of real Jamaican jerk chicken here on the island of Jamaica-

I am presently eating while fleeting thoughts are being salvaged for this piece of literature- for documentation I planted a thumb print of sauce in my journal where I expected to be writing of this mouth watering event however one does not contain or can sum up a spring once it begins flowing and so it was placed a bit prematurely further up on the page but just as I was jotting this confession, my page was seasoned once again – the result of a carelessly yet blissful bite of Jamaican jerk chicken, so now here at this point on the page the sauce lies staining purely by an accidental arrival .... Is not that just how life mocks, how life shows its *life* by its poetic irony its unpredictable capability to just make it happen right when it should and not a moment sooner-

In this state I eat and appreciate eating most I feel free in a freedom where any type of oppression would have to be searched for and I'm not moving-

Anyone who observes would surely envy... reaching for a *piece* of their own to obtain the taste that seems so clearly perfect-

What they fail to realize is that it has taken days for me to adapt -taken the hours of before to just sway involuntarily to the resonance of the steel drum the sweet soft sound of the Caribbean riff and still I know it's not to my glory nor to my own self training or observations of social sciences, no more than a chameleon has slowly taught himself to notice objects differing in color only then to put in himself that difference and becoming it, placing into thin air the color he was before, it is the Divine designer *Who* has done this thing-

It is Him *who* has done for me as well and so at this moment it is God I have to thank for I truly realize it is He who gives this to me as a foreshadowing- a confirmation of His will and purpose for little ole me-

However the exhilaration comes as I find myself alone, as this is the usual enigma of my nirvana- resist your urge to rush off with Mr. opinion, it has been shared and witnessed confirming my sanity still the majority- the most of its beauty has only one intimate observer... The Holy Ghost-

I have not just been sitting back letting my red neck spread to the other regions of the state of Joshua while drinking down piña coladas and filling my bowels with chicken smothered in jerk sauce setting myself up for a spicy aftermath in the little boys room – Dad would be so jealous.

I have had my fill and I have laid back for how else does one take in what is not already within -I must observe I must ponder I must look with intent and become all, so too I have digested some of this people, so too may I win a few-

I have collected some Intel for my great escape – I am fully aware how all this would seem to so many as if I am only parading around in this fantasy in my head bound to this folly of insignificant work that does not resemble work at all because of its seasons differing in need but you must remember I am caught in the middle, in the middle of societies church and the Church between the working class rodent race and ministering truth between resort and native conditions between adventure and *responsibility* between death and life.... So do try to understand I am trying to bring much of this Way away from the beaten path it has its contradictions and it has its resentments yet I see the importance and God has graced me with no other choice and that is truly gracious to me as I am overwhelmed with choice –

So now where were we oh yes digesting people well that's just it I understand a bit of what I have eaten, like us their condition in the spirit could use enlightening-To the men in Athens Greece leisure time was spent talking, they talked of every wind of doctrine that blew through, any new thought they would speak of, so when Paul came through he spoke philosophy deeply and profoundly, so authentic in statement some of them there said- what is this babbling fool trying to say – think for a moment what he must have sounded like to them- his philosophy was not just a thought but a complete explanation of every thing, able to maintain the very reason for life, I have heard some that made such attempts of explaining their take on life they do so with an energy, full to the brim of their own emotion and shamelessly spewing it all over the listener, as if they have to rush through it and be so intense as if to be squeezing it into the very structure of life at least they are trying to squeeze it into my head because they actually know how difficult an undertaking it is to explain something that would then explain everything – I can not help but imagine this is how Paul appeared to them these men so accustomed to hearing and telling – some of these philosophers listened and heard an axiom and one so magnificently maintained – allow me to paraphrase.... God the one creator over all things One you do not know to name because you know you know Him not yet a plaque testifies the reservation for you men of thought to think once more, now think of this, One who is in everything because He has given life to everything, the source of life dwelling in all life and even more giving life everlasting- Here in Jamaica these things are emphasized-love-respect-beauty-and life.

Enjoying each other and the earth we stand upon and God whom it all depends- Yet to put this all together they tried perhaps short handedly to set a religion for it -Rasta- To unify- to preserve they ordained for themselves this order, however because of the lack of knowledge they fell into the holes of an illusive doctrine yet zeal should be congratulated- this is not an evil people and where they lack we too have an equally intense tragedy within our misconceptions and the consequence there of- So do not judge lest you be judged- they have great attributes and if your attributes provide you able to enlighten to fill in the holes with firm truth ...start shoveling It's a funny thing how thought comes together like waves to the beach molding stones, pulling loose sand to the depths and weight of the oceanic- It seems the natives to this land were comprised of two people the Tainos and the Carribs the Carribs are no longer here they were a murderous people who constantly hunted men to eat them, anyway the Spanish showed up and put a stop to this menacing unwavering people and completely cut them off, the Tainos probably hoped for somebody to show up and kill the Spanish but it didn't happen they were enslaved so harshly the race was nearly lost, other slaves from Africa would be shipped in to pick up the slack-

My fascination is this... Christ said unless you eat of my flesh and drink of my blood you can not live- These Carribs ate others to live stealing from them their lives and devouring their very flesh causing people to have great fear and focus on killing every last one of them- Yet this Jesus offered His own body to be eaten, consumed for the souls of the partakers to have life and life more abundantly, quite the reverse- So this be my last day I be leavin the island tomorrow mon leavin the Caribbean's Surely there's enough page for just one more thought...... So here's what I'm thinking maybe the Carribs are not completely gone maybe a few went into hiding and the bloodline exists today, they do still claim the title of the place- After all you are what you eat-

FOR IF WE SHARE IN HIS DEATH WE WILL SHARE IN HIS RESURRECTION

LOVE AND RESPECT MON FROM JAMAICA

EXILES

To the world assembled in one place, those who claim, willing and enlightened
To those whom God has sealed, prophets sent with and without restrain
where are the lines, exiled and forgotten faiths, the walls, temples and foreign saints
is it all a stupid dream-
The casual, indecent acts of charade
Under the garment zeal chipped away
Son of man write what you see
Is it all a stupid dream-

THE COLD

The cold has returned- Its silence
Instantly I am reminded
its days pass slowly
There along the way of the stream I ask myself many things
The emptiness of its night
for miles it carries a lone wave of sound
Its silence falls deep into the ravine
I am found low beside its moving current
I will take some water
the cold will breathe through the night
All will drop into that void
all of tonight
hour by hour
Candle after candle
my pot of water will boil
My master will bathe
the cold will overcome
The steam- The flame- The hour.

SUNDAY MORNING

Sunday morning it's cold in the room
I'm cold, Lord God give me comfort
bearing guilt within the cloud for I love the storm and the whirlwind
originality with every sensation the Ghost ministers to my being
to feel the Helper here allows me to trust the true assembly
still even among witnesses of the eternal living
vulcanized spirits come between daughters and sons mothers and
fathers
disappointments driven hard by dissatisfying the appetite of
expectation
followed with prayers and anointment, spring divided brackish water
still we strive and continue and for that we will achieve-
laurel wreath- purple ribbon
a time to breathe deeply, warmed by the rays of God from the
throne of majesty-
will we follow close enough to the Son- so to know well the Holy
Ghost
will the mystic truth of the Christian be shared with every spirit's host

LOVES

I seek a place to be just to be... lovers are taking us too serious. I am put to shame- I am ashamed where did that time pass onto, where did we get off refusing the river its drift why must we be ashamed, why does the beast always escape, to death I ponder so cursed I scream to tell the devil he's a serpent yet I am a snake. My soul needs water sleeping awake my heart needs love dying to breathe gasp another day, another friend we leave in the end.

Many are the divided river ways they run to oceans eternities.

I am tired of myself and everyone else- I'm in obsessive love with everyone else roses of flowers darkest of powers why are the women beautifully bright why is my heart a lying dark light.

Days, days, days the wind does not always blow the days are not always a glow, some only pass us by.

Loves you are too many for me, loves save the petals before the last one falls, the tears don't come at all, let us run into the forest as the leaves drop and we will stop out there and not worry as the sun descends we will be in peace not afraid not lost not blinded by the dark. But together at last all of us together at last.

- Joshua
Joseph

Part Two

THE ADMONISHMENT

THE MEANING OF THE TEACHER'S SORROW

I am the one you speak to while you're waiting for someone else; the one you say the things you're not quite positive about, but still forming your opinion on a matter. The freedom you have with me is different than your other relationships. I welcome you to come and go. We are more than acquaintances, much more, but less than a devoted pair. You keep it that way to keep from annoyance; to give my word a chance to sink in deep to where you can't remember source, but are propelled to choose nobly; having chosen truth above self and its ambitious works. Why then can't I be embraced like one with folly bound within? Why can't the true be excepted by the ones they edify? Can I not break from being a nuisance... or is that the way one is made better? Though my credit is not given by you, but from the one who gives on account of man's heart. Do not say in your mind, he wants praise; he wants to be attended to for his works.

I would only like to be accepted for what I am; and the fruit being good should also be accepted. This cannot be shown in gesture or grin; these things deceive; more, the cold fraction from friend to teacher; how impersonal and distant is this chosen method of learning. Teach me. Now, leave me so you do not see how I choose to put truth into action, so you do not see if I honor what I seem to honor. Away now, so that I can decide comfortably after the echo of your words have passed from me, and also those who have seen you speak them. First the teacher is taught, then he sees; and what he sees, he learns. He sees more than what he himself teaches, else his well would run dry. No, he sees how his words enter, and how they are felt in the student's receiver. Students are anyone who is listening to a teacher. Whether they know it or not. They are students. There are temporary students and devout, all learn, some despise, most recent; but all that which is rejected is not the teacher... it is the truth! To tell the truth is to be responded to with lies. Out of courtesy when you are honest, man will repay you with blatant deceit to protect themselves, of course. Pride aids in the survival of the ego to protect that beautiful appearance of knowing everything. Wisdom is gained through the realization and acceptance of one's own ignorance.

APOSTLES, PROPHETS, EVANGELISTS, PASTORS, AND TEACHERS

We make the mistake thinking, let us put him here under this tradition and here to fulfill this role; however the Spirit that is in us is alive, creative and bold.

Do not squeeze a man, born again, into the mold of another; he lives to fulfill his own destiny, one for God. Instead we put them in the usual places of the church and when they do not find themselves truly dedicated to the norm we pass blame and judge their shortcomings as a lack of discipline and even passion, even if he were lacking and was a weak believer -

"Who are you to pass judgment on the servant of another? It is before his own master that he stands or falls. And he will be upheld, for the Lord is able to make him stand."

The irony; scripturally, the weak believer is the one with the rigid system of faith and the stronger faith is not bound by man's tradition.

Our churches have become platforms for only a few type of workmen instead of a fellowship of believers sharing in the same Spirit, the same Love, and the Liberty to produce Fruits for the Kingdom.

Jesus the Author of our faith does not pen predictable script nor is He amused by our robotic means to produce fruit, a denomination's agenda, or a local church mission statement, but instead let each man have his own agenda one called and authored by God, called into being by the present need to edify the Church, a called into calling, a more personal connection with the Divine and confirmed by a daily assurance that he the individual is firstly promoted by the Promised Holy Ghost and secondly supported by the True Assembly for the ministry of Jesus Christ.

Give the Christian soldier a home not a building with a steeple marking its exclusive right to uphold the practices we have collected throughout the centuries of civil man while losing grip of the Gifts and Commandments of God that He has imparted to His Eternal Society. To the peculiar treasure in clay pots the customs of the church way heavy on their heart and the ritual of elders discourages the newness God may bring through certain types of individuals, if the individual is convinced his or her unique spirit is unable to be used in the congregation or even worst is misunderstood as an unclean offering, then the believer and his or her contribution are both unaccepted and mistrusted. And all this for the sake of containing power and control.

Let us scratch the name of leaders from our minds, follow Jesus in the Spirit and walk together.

Do I mean to say some should not be acknowledged as prophet, guide or leader, no, but if we have in our dictum that leader is one who leads by upholding tradition, as if tradition had for itself guards, well then this service is a lifeless pursuit and will only lead towards regular behavior.

Regular behavior is having us remain as we are, non progressive, contained, and keeping outsiders away by a stigma that is more than relevant due to the uniformity of our ways on the sun's day.

It is interesting to think what we would display if solely governed by Gods commandments and Christ fulfillment of the law, love. Why do we trade Divine Revelation for formal conduct, why trade Spiritual Illumination for the routine, and how do we usher out the old and welcome the unknown.

Why do we limit the gifts of God and make few what He has varied; and when did The Church become just church?

What we have in the present is a derivative of the former disclosures concerning the church, here is what I mean, within the scriptures are our precepts, our knowledge and while some aspects are quite clear and admittedly unfulfilled others are left up for interpretation and as a result not practiced at all. I will share this example to help further explain, while studying about Palestine I came across an interesting thought, it concerned the boundaries of the Promised Land God had given to the Hebrew nation, though God himself gave this land to His people the parameters were not clearly established, a history of warfare that exists today provides painful evidence, my thought however was this "That which is not clearly defined is meant for battle. "Scripture paired with eyes to see is more than adequate in supplying us with all truth; Still with some issues one must work harder to repossess an order, this may be due to translation, time, various winds of doctrine, modern structures or values contrasting with biblical ethic, or a limited scripture basis. In our case all of the above. Scriptures surrounding this are few and so much is built and respected on one or two references, if nothing else this hinders perspective and breeds unnecessary absolutes. The word pastor is used only once in the New Testament, it is found in the letter to the Ephesians, *a gift of the Holy Spirit, He Christ appointed men to shepherd and lead.* <u>Now with this position others are stated as well and that's one key,</u> another point is the term pastor, this was not used as an official title in the early Church, what I mean by that is it was not an occupation of sorts or a singular office of head leadership.

<u>Another interesting point is the term shepherd is used interchangeably with messengers, servants, watchmen and even prophets throughout the Holy Scriptures.</u>

And so I fear it was Christ's intention that we have sacrificed.

A true leader are those who can interpret the Divine Will of God or one who supports and guides the people that way, by refreshing, expounding, exposing, <u>and most importantly following the Divine Will of God</u>, allowing himself to be a mere echo of our Lord's voice in the present age.

This scripture is a short list to the Ephesians leaving out the supernatural manifestations mentioned in the letter to the Corinthians but opening with *"[His gifts were varied: He Himself appointed and gave men to us]"*

These men or gifts or types of men are ***apostles, prophets, evangelists, pastors, and teachers*** and so in essence men were given **these gifts as gifts** to the Church, then and till the end of this age. Christ's intention is clear in verse twelve and thirteen *"His intention was the perfecting and the full equipping of the saints (His consecrated people), [that they should do] the work of ministering toward building up Christ's body (the church),[That it might develop] until we all attain oneness in the faith and in the comprehension of the [full and accurate] knowledge of the Son of God, that [we might arrive] at really mature* *manhood (the completeness of personality which is nothing less than the standard height of Christ's own perfection), the measure of the stature of the fullness of the Christ and the completeness found in Him.*

What we have done is taken one of these purposed leaders and placed on him all the expectation and authority to deliver a complete leading.

This has misled us to non biblical ideals that have been shattered only to be pieced back together so many times that our work is powered by human effort to uphold a human misunderstanding, a corporate system actually betraying the personal commitment intended to be shared by brothers, if Jesus was the first born then we now are many, yet I am reserved as layman and you are used up as clergy, why is there this mentality, am I not a slave as you? Did I not count the cost as you? Have I not laid aside my own passions for Christ to live and me to die? As if being ordained is a human affair as we have made it, those being humanly qualified receive blind respect and for the other brethren, they must pay their dues as a proper worker of the Kingdom ought. As if my qualifications could be found at the end of much study and earned credentials, as Paul tells the Church at Corinth.... *ARE WE starting to commend ourselves again? Or we do not, like some [false teachers], need written credentials or letters of recommendation to you or from you, [do we]? [No] you yourselves are our letter of recommendation (our credentials), written in your hearts, to be known (perceived, recognized) and read by everybody. You show and make obvious that you are a letter from Christ delivered by us, not written with ink but with [the] Spirit of [the] living God, not on tablets of stone but on tablets of human hearts.]*

Our credentials are to be the fruit we bear through prudent, and persistent effort made towards the edification of our own spirit and mind and for the spirit and mind of our brothers and sisters, this fruit is seen and shared through the assembly and makes real our individual spiritual identity within the Kingdom.

Being partial to this mentality of high priest is not new, many religious systems had a high priest and coming from a Jewish origin I suppose Christianity had it coming, the Roman Catholic Empire did not help fight against adopting this methodology but embraced it completely. Israel experienced for themselves the move from spirituality to religion, their elders formed the ruling aristocracy and had for itself a high priest, from this party we see the dogmatic, Pharisaical mind set we like to distance ourselves from. This is a political fashion for upholding our perception of a necessary order.

In the letter to Timothy much is described by Paul concerning an appearance of godliness, I will show only two verses in the context read for yourselves the chapter but these two will serve well enough,

1 Timothy 6:5-6 [And protracted wrangling and wearing discussion and perpetual friction among men who are corrupted in mind and bereft of

the truth, who imagine that godliness or righteousness is a [-*source of profit [a moneymaking business, a means of livelihood]. From such withdraw. 6[And it is, indeed, a source of immense profit, for] godliness accompanied with contentment (that contentment which is a sense of (inward sufficiency) is great and abundant gain.*

The position of pastor has been made of singular importance, and even acquiring for itself a form of business and or livelihood as an undisputed norm. Furthermore deeming one office chiefly and misunderstanding the other parts of leadership will not make up a whole but will create for itself a facade, refusing the variations will cause gross proportion to one member of the Body. The letter to the Corinthians describes the immaturity of putting some over others in superiority.

1Cor.4:6-7

6Now I have applied all this [about parties and factions] to myself and Apollos for your sakes, brethren, so that from what I have said of us [as illustrations], you may learn [to think of men in accordance with Scripture and] not to go beyond that which is written, that none of you may be puffed up and inflated with pride and boast in favor of one [minister and teacher] against another.

7For who separates you from the others [as a faction leader]? [Who makes you superior and sets you apart from another, giving you the preeminence?] What have you that was not given to you? If then you received it [from someone], why do you boast as if you had not received [but had gained it by your own efforts]?

Our contemporary church has for itself a capitalistic system, to the point of incorporating, and in any corporation there are offices to be held, a presidential position a vice president and so on, my point is for so many this is no surprise and seems strange for me to even mention, however these systems are man made, democratic, American, ways of governing. Democratic because the people choose leaders for themselves, American because that is our loved ideal, some of us have more pride in country than God's Kingdom or have been deceived in thinking America is to be defended for it is an upright nation founded on Christian values when really most of the world's civil societies have always shared common values and still rejected God, hate to tell you but if America the beautiful is still a nation in the end days it too will be surrounding Israel, and the birds of the air will feed on its highly esteemed soldiers and generals as well as the rest. As a democratic church we decide for God who leads, also those few decide for God what their campaign shall be remembered for, sounds like the white house doesn't it? A president is not what God gave the Church as a guide; He appointed for Himself a varied few to simply be a medium for the development of the Body to achieve oneness. What we have is a modern system of rule and order sharing sympathies with the world's sophistication rather than the New Testament Scriptures and its Kingdom principles.

So that there should be no division or discord or lack of adaptation [of the parts of the body to each other], but the members all alike should have a mutual interest in and care for one another. **Paul to the Corinthians-**

The Church has for itself many parts that make up the whole, each one being vital and needed for the proper condition the Lord designed for His Eternal Nation, this Nation had its means of operation already, offices which were even given titles of their own and yet we have taken it upon ourselves to replace these truths with the ways of man, the traditions of man, why do we do this? Jesus claimed that man, religious man, Pharisee, chooses to fulfill the tradition of man rather than the commandments of God.

APOSTLES, PROPHETS, EVANGELISTS, PASTORS, AND TEACHERS, PART TWO OF TWO *THE HOLY GHOST IN US AND IN THE CHURCH*

I dropped the first letter on both my pastors' desks, one did not respond at all and the other simply handed me a bunch of papers he printed out, these were from his denominations library of doctrines and bylaws. I looked at the first page, *"The Christian and Missionary Alliance statement on "church government"*; Need I say more.

I have been sort of bothered by this all day, I can't figure out why someone would need to deal with me or my writing so impersonally. I tried to begin writing Part Two bearing the title above but would wander back in thought to the way Part One was received; I felt this introduction would be a more genuine way to deal with what is happening and.... good journalism., well not completely, it did dawn on me as to the WHY.... I do believe I have realized.

I now believe, the present day pastor is not concerned with revelations concerning scripture on "church government" and why should they be, their on top. I suppose I was kidding myself thinking all new creatures were interested in the *coming completion of the age* and the Word, the Word being with God and the Word being God.

Before I get carried away let me disclose what my curiosity or neurosis rather led me to understand- first, a spiritual man is to test all things yet it seems better for some to settle on a denomination's bylaws; to go about doing the work of Christ with them in place, so to go on without arguing precepts, being in harmony and agreement hoping for the power and peace that comes from organization; an organization.

Thus making a denomination's doctrine off limits!

One would quickly distance himself from a Pharisee- or a Pharisaical lifestyle however many would be surprised to hear the faith these men professed both in the resurrection and of angels, basically.... they did so much as to believe in the unseen realm., So, one more accurately would distance themselves from the resemblance of the Sadducee., the point is the Pharisee believed there was a spirit realm but did not eagerly pursue its benefits. Also one could deduce that the Pharisee who favors the traditions of man is fine with the revelations concerning the unseen realm.

Consider what we do have in regard to leadings- is it then to the divine will of God or by a sort of papal office.? Divinity is seen and established through the workings of the Holy Ghost- this was promised by Jesus and was the evidence of Truth in the Church., so why no more,? Well.... perhaps I can disclose a reason., one miss of a scripture having to do with the inner workings of the assembly leads to a false doctrine and a complete misconception of core truths concerning the very context and implications of that scripture- watch here- as a modern fellowship we have placed the supernatural manifestations of the Holy Spirit as a secondary mechanism, a mere peripheral, a tool that comes and goes without certitude or absolution., plainly said- something we could all do without. And we have done without, anyone could see that- yet the scripture permanently states the reason and importance of supernatural energy and is beautifully expressed in Hebrews the second chapter, here are a few of those verses:

"SINCE ALL this is true, we ought to pay much closer attention than ever to the truths that we have heard, lest in any way we drift past [them] and slip away.

For if the message given through angels [the Law spoken by them to Moses] was authentic and proved sure, and every violation and disobedience received an appropriate (just and adequate) penalty,

How shall we escape [appropriate retribution] if we neglect and refuse to pay attention to such a great salvation [as is now offered to us, letting it drift past us forever]? For it was declared at first by the Lord [Himself], and it was confirmed to us and proved to be real and genuine by those who personally heard [Him speak].

[Besides this evidence] it was also established and plainly endorsed by God, Who showed His approval of it by signs and wonders and various miraculous manifestations of [His] power and by imparting the gifts of the Holy Spirit [to the believers] according to His own will.

For it was not to angels that God subjected the habitable world of the future, of which we are speaking.

It has been solemnly and earnestly said in a certain place, What is man that You are mindful of him, or the son of man that You graciously and helpfully care for and visit and look after him?

For some little time You have ranked him lower than and inferior to the angels; You have crowned him with glory and honor and set him over the works of Your hands, For You have put everything in subjection under his feet. Now in putting everything in subjection to man, He left nothing outside [of man's] control. But at present we do not yet see all things subjected to him [man].

But we are able to see Jesus, Who was ranked lower than the angels for a little while, crowned with glory and honor because of His having suffered death, in order that by the grace (unmerited favor) of God [to us sinners] He might experience death for every individual person."

A power struggle occurs when one party's use of power conflicts with another party's use of power, except in the True Church- there is no single person's exclusive right to receive- The Power - In the beginning God created man, earth and creatures- man was given dominance- given power- man therefore desires power and naturally so- it is his natural inheritance and so his authority is given by God. Every religion seeks this_ in the Church we all are to have power, each differing and also compiling to further the Kingdom in good warfare, warring against darkness, hastening the coming of Christ. What we have instead are a few having power due to an earthly decree or qualifying factor- the rest of the fellowship being fed sedatives and kept at bay; worst yet kept from the promised Holy Spirit- the head of a religious office always secures this monopoly- not so with the true Church where a commune of saints possess the Spirit, it motivates all who are involved and unbelievers are brought to sight through signs of the supernatural- all this is demonstrated in the Word but has been made out to be problematic- really the Church is to display a **harmony of power** to a world that knows no such thing. This contribution is to be a testament, one to our new being, giving back what we have freely received., once this is perceived there is no argument, it becomes obvious how incredibly vital the **Spirit is to the Body**), the Individual, THE GOSPEL, THE KINGDOM'S ETRERNITY **for scripture claims** *"for by the Holy Spirit we have our life in God"* - If this is undermined in any way.... well, one can only imagine what has been compromised- concerning the role of the Holy Spirit, His most central importance, gifts, fruits- and all these holding the biblical entitlement as **evidence**., thus compromising evidence.

I have learned it is a misconception that leads to dogma-

In the letter to the Corinthians Paul is expounding on the gift of tongues, prophesy,, order. Studying these verses proved frustrating for a time, the words forming sentences forming context seemed an obvious contradiction, still I knew it was not as it seemed, I just knew the secret was there hiding, it was right there in the text waiting to spring up, as all the angles were being explored like a single person in a crowd- you scan and scan until they just pop up, you know instantly you have found what you were searching for.

It reads:

"Thus [unknown] tongues are meant for a [supernatural] sign, not for believers but for unbelievers [on the point of believing], while prophecy (inspired preaching and teaching, interpreting the divine will and purpose) is not for unbelievers [on the point of believing] but for believers.

Therefore, if the whole church assembles and all of you speak in [unknown] tongues, and the ungifted and uninitiated or unbelievers come in, will they not say that you are demented?

But if all prophesy [giving inspired testimony and interpreting the divine will and purpose] and an unbeliever or untaught outsider comes in, he is told of his sin and reproved and convicted and convinced by all, and his defects and needs are examined (estimated, determined) and he is called to account by all,

The secrets of his heart are laid bare; and so, falling on [his] face, he will worship God, declaring that God is among you in very truth.

What then, brethren, is [the right course]? When you meet together, each one has a hymn, a teaching, a disclosure of special knowledge or information, an utterance in a [strange] tongue, or an interpretation of it. [But] let everything be constructive and edifying and for the good of all.

If some speak in a [strange] tongue, let the number be limited to two or at the most three, and each one [taking his] turn, and let one interpret and explain [what is said].

But if there is no one to do the interpreting, let each of them keep still in church and talk to himself and to God.

So let two or three prophets speak [those inspired to preach or teach], while the rest pay attention and weigh and discern what is said.

But if an inspired revelation comes to another who is sitting by, then let the first one be silent.

For in this way you can give testimony [prophesying and thus interpreting the divine will and purpose] one by one, so that all may be instructed and all may be stimulated and encouraged;

For the spirits of the prophets (the speakers in tongues) are under the speaker's control [and subject to being silenced as may be necessary], For He [Who is the source of their prophesying] is not a God of confusion and disorder but of peace and order. As [is the practice] in all the churches of the saints (God's people),"

When it struck my consciousness I realized the issue Paul had faced was a matter of **order**. Typically a staunch perspective even rule is derived from this scripture, it goes as follows: an unknown tongue ought not to be uttered if there is no interpreter- which is sensible,....scriptural and I can sympathize and have even rebuked others according to this ideal though it seemed to carry a sort of legalism with it which I never cared for, except it seemed to make most sense regarding this controversial issue and so I adopted this view- however once realizing the fullness I am now joyful enacting what I see as the truth of the matter- the matter in it's entirety has more to do with order in expressing the Divine character of God- in carefully displaying the spiritual illumination- being the representation of God.- first of all, **a tongue must be spoken out in faith before an interpretation can follow**, that's practical enough; just as others should weigh out a prophesy they too should interpret a tongue.... it carries through from prophets prophesying in order one at a time while the other prophets weigh and discern what is spoken- this tone does not change but enriches as Paul follows through with the speaking of tongues, he discloses actual truth, the consequence of prophesy of hearing a tongue- and here is the main point: there is no contradiction though he does state tongues are a sign to an unbeliever; he is specific in ordering that all the assembly not speak at once whether in an unknown tongue or a known tongue, makes no difference- his example is verse twenty three beginning with (**therefore**) and connecting all that was said before. We have it wrong in thinking some gifts are more hooky spooky than others; if a word is taught in the knowledge of the Divine will of God this is a supernatural happening; and we sit every Sunday and listen to words spoken in our tongue as if God himself wants us to hear what is being said- except this is all we allow time and authority for besides song- and in song there is barely the freedom and creativity the Spirit affords- **the Letter reads a song- a hymn- a tongue- a word-** we routinely follow the week before rather than the Word, this is not <u>true fellowship,</u> this is an organized attempt to revere piety- The unchallenged role of a pastor is much of the problem and knowing the upset that statement may cause I still must go on- we should openly decide and understand whether we will go on showing up for one man's ministry or for all of our ministries- not to say we need fight for Sunday, we have every day of the week to minister and revere God- we are not bound to a Sabbath day but are free to deem everyday holy- Sunday being Sabbath is as much a problem as the building being church.

Paul charges Timothy to **preach**- correcting, rebuking, teaching, doing the work of an evangelist- I adore what God spoke to the young Timothy through Paul:

"[So] that in Him in every respect you were enriched, in full power and readiness of speech [to speak of your faith] and complete knowledge and illumination [to give you full insight into its meaning]."

We handover our responsibilities and forfeit our gifts our powers to the establishments man giving them all authority which belongs to Christ who is head of the Body- **fellowship is living together** not formalities- fellowship is helping each other not holding out for a professional to arrive- fellowship is equal and freedom provides a comfortable approach to just be- an instrument, a vessel to show God's power- the Holy Spirit ought guide us to repentance- fulfillment- outpouring- intimacy-

Given to help us bring about our very destiny a destiny bound together.

PRIMITIVE CHRISTIANITY COMPARED TO CHRISTIAN MODERNISM

I wonder what many of you would think of these verses- how you would reason and fit modern times with the Holiness of Scripture-;

For those who want to learn truth we have the Scriptures

For those who want to learn boldness we apply those truths

Conclusion-: Anyone who lives a Godly life will be persecuted.

The Scripture itself powerfully states a force to fight against-

Jesus is the Word.) The original realist- THE GREAT I AM

The scriptures speak for itself, The Word after all is The Word-

Only be contemplative and still, inherit the characteristics of being born again-

I am complete, in Christ I have obtained all and have my fullness-

Realizing man's deceit and forsaking the fulfillment of his demands-

AND NOW THE WORD

"See to it that no one carries you off as spoil or makes you yourselves captive by his so-called philosophy and intellectualism and vain deceit (idle fancies and plain nonsense), following human tradition (men's ideas of the material rather than the spiritual world), just crude notions following the rudimentary and elemental teachings of the universe and disregarding [the teachings of] Christ (the Messiah).

And you are in Him, made full and having come to fullness of life [in Christ you too are filled with the Godhead--Father, Son and Holy Spirit--and reach full spiritual stature]. And He is the Head of all rule and authority [of every angelic principality and power].

In Him also you were circumcised with a circumcision not made with hands, but in a [spiritual] circumcision [performed by] Christ by stripping off the body of the flesh (the whole corrupt, carnal nature with its passions and lusts)

Having cancelled and blotted out and wiped away the handwriting of the note (bond) with its legal decrees and demands which was in force and stood against us (hostile to us). This [note with its regulations, decrees, and demands] He set aside and cleared completely out of our way by nailing it to [His] cross.

[God] disarmed the principalities and powers that were ranged against us and made a bold display and public example of them, in triumphing over them in Him and in it [the cross].

Therefore let no one sit in judgment on you in matters of food and drink, or with regard to a feast day or a New Moon or a Sabbath.

Such [things] are only the shadow of things that are to come, and they have only a symbolic value. But the reality (the substance, the solid fact of what is foreshadowed, the body of it) belongs to Christ.

Let no one defraud you by acting as an umpire and declaring you unworthy and disqualifying you for the prize, insisting on self-abasement and worship of angels, taking his stand on visions [he claims] he has seen, vainly puffed up by his sensuous notions and inflated by his unspiritual thoughts and fleshly conceit, and not holding fast to the Head, from Whom the entire body, supplied and knit together by means of its joints and ligaments, grows with a growth that is from God.

If then you have died with Christ to material ways of looking at things and have escaped from the world's crude and elemental notions and teachings of externalism, why do you live as if you still belong to the world? [Why do you submit to rules and regulations?--such as]

Do not handle [this], Do not taste [that], Do not even touch [them], Referring to things all of which perish with being used. To do this is to follow human precepts and doctrines.

Such [practices] have indeed the outward appearance [that popularly passes] for wisdom, in promoting self-imposed rigor of devotion and delight in self-humiliation and severity of discipline of the body, but they are of no value in checking the indulgence of the flesh (the lower nature). [Instead, they do not honor God but serve only to indulge the flesh.]

IF THEN you have been raised with Christ [to a new life, thus sharing His resurrection from the dead], aim at and seek the [rich, eternal treasures] that are above, where Christ is, seated at the right hand of God.

And set your minds and keep them set on what is above (the higher things), not on the things that are on the earth.

For [as far as this world is concerned] you have died, and your [new, real] life is hidden with Christ in God.

And let the peace (soul harmony which comes) from Christ rule (act as umpire continually) in your hearts [deciding and settling with finality all questions that arise in your minds, in that peaceful state] to which as [members of Christ's] one body you were also called [to live]. And be thankful (appreciative), [giving praise to God always].

Let the word [spoken by] Christ (the Messiah) have its home [in your hearts and minds] and dwell in you in [all its] richness, as you teach and admonish and train one another in all insight and intelligence and wisdom [in spiritual things, and as you sing] psalms and hymns and spiritual songs, making melody to God with [His] grace in your hearts

Let your speech at all times be gracious (pleasant and winsome), seasoned [as it were] with salt, [so that you may never be at a loss] to know how you ought to answer anyone [who puts a question to you]."

A HOLY WAR AGAINST MODERNISM Continues with this-

I begin with a question; have we at all made the Jews jealous yet? We have the Jewish people to thank for our salvation, yes that's right., the Holy Scriptures state this spiritual fact- have you not heard it said that salvation comes from the Jews.

God in all His wisdom granted us blessing, favor and eternal life free of charge without the dogmatic ritualistic lifestyle of the Jew., the Jewish guidelines were enforced by the entire community- it was very much at its core a social force- which led to its vanity- it was in the end pronounced by Jesus as hypocrisy- God revealed to men that their necessary ways to holiness were no longer necessary and that all who would believe in obedience that Jesus is Lord would be saved, receiving blessing- inheritance- favor- ***will be envied*** by men.

With this knowledge comes the examination of church culture-who we are- how we live-our guidelines- I do not hide my view within words but will state plainly that our entanglement is evident., thus we need to break free to live in the light of the new day- this freedom should transcend our times. To think that God would use jealousy to invoke His will is to say the least fascinating to me and within these thoughts I go beyond the fulfillment of the chosen people being grafted back into the tree of life and ponder for a moment..... if this jealousy can win the heart of a religious man to the eternal truth and mystery of life then what affect could it have on a wandering gentile- unbelievers look at the church and generally see a culture of people and those people do not seem at all extraordinary- and I will dare tell you why; We have misrepresented the very foundation of our new life the life we all share together-and we expect to be as living stones built into a spiritual house but built on what foundation. **The true and firm foundation is to be represented as one stone, One Living Stone... The Truths The Sacrifice The Resurrection Power of Jesus The Christ. The very stone the builders rejected has become the chief cornerstone.** No other stones are needed in this foundation, our church claims to have this one foundation ..... so do thousands of denominations from the extremely perverse to the *"bible based "*assemblies., all claim this foundation but add many more stones to their foundation until it rises to become a wall... a penitentiary is formed and vibes are generated from the very construction: A people are held inside these walls and a people are kept outside- These walls we create or at the least inherit and defend are cultures. We don't mean it, so many of us do not even understand the complexities of sociology but strangely without understanding it cultures are formed and recognized for their tolerances and attitudes- we believe quite highly of ourselves and we should we are children of the King however those outside the kingdom are not seeing what sets us apart- to them we are simply a smaller part of man's society, the conservative part to be exact- they see a people guided by the whim of the status quo, our concern with status is earthly non spiritual and a terrible witness to our liberty and the fullness we have in Christ, we voluntarily bog each other down with the concerns of the world and enforce strictly notions we perceive as proper with the power of social pressure, ashamedly believers are obligated to obey as these notions go untested as an authentic **Holy Precept**. Unbelievers do not want to join a cloud of witnesses that will hold them to the common traits of civilized man- This is a hollow cast- a trivial venture., bound to tire and drive a true seeker into the desert for a time to reflect purely without a tainted audience- Our obligation is not to uphold modern ways of living instead we are to surpass all time, all heritage and even our own flesh; Safeguarding tradition will only bring about a most immature conduct that will prove singlehandedly that we use the name of Jesus to only secure our own pursuit of happiness- Our standards of living should be a profound paradox encouraging the blind to open their eyes, to look far past the expectations of man and serve a living God. Our partialities are weakness, immense weakness that breaks us down at the most fundamental levels of fellowship- active prejudice occur whenever the most basic liberty is exercised, and the unbeliever chooses his unbelief for yet another day- communion is undermined and the individual loses perspective on personal relations with Jesus and the brethren, no meaning no fulfillment only a routine that the world itself portrays, the cycle seems to go on forever- and the culture is one, a single cell, all doing the same thing the same way and so looking forward to the next *occasion*- except the cell the harmony is not to bond to this cause- no- not this purpose; for what purpose is it to be on time, to have structure, to sit down, stand up bow your head, now close your eyes. We are aliens- yes immigrants this is not our home these are not our ways, our ways are foreign, otherworldly- we must shed all our coats in good courage and reveal the one born of the Spirit that it may testify of the Stone, the One Stone the builders rejected, it has become Chief Cornerstone, we must trust all our lives **will** stay supported, we must be singular and know He is faithful and true.

We no longer need the ways of man we have The Messiah to guide us into all Truth, If we trust entirely in Him we will produce in His creative power- and will display an unprecedented right of passage- and that is what this is all about **rights of passage** – people will want the right to all God entitles them to, in seeing it granted to us- and granted on one basis- CHRIST- **THE SWORD OF DIVISION IS CHRIST'S ALONE**

LAST SUNDAY OR THE PREACHER'S HOPE

I sat with my ear inclined – to the man, to the preacher – I then called attention to all the neurons to come together in submissive concentration to the will and knowledge of Christ- My eyes forward – fixed on the figure stationed behind the pulpit- the altar for sacrifice and offering of words – the white synthetic canvas loomed overhead of the preacher and without notice appeared a carefully chosen quote from a clever little monk, the first of subject matter, It generally stated that no angelic visitation nor any vision can be compared to the scripture itself. It hit me like a dart, a small piercing but it was strongly felt - this was a subtle offense inserted especially against the mystical element of our experience with Christ and to the present strengthening of the assemblies faith against supernatural interruptions to our perfect lives while studying the WORD – as I refocused I heard the why -the what – the preacher's hope – The preacher's hope both pure and just with spiritual and practical importance rendering immeasurable consequence – one that would cause the walls of our church building to burst outward spewing us all over the ground – and as we lift ourselves up seeing the collection of saints differing so we would leave the rubble at once to fish for men; calling them to repentance and faith in Jesus as Lord – this hope is that we the people would know the Word, first, and go off preaching second – this is a great hope – Why though, to show and teach this great thing would we bash another of God's works?

How could you say or allow another man to quote the scripture's superiority to supernatural happenings ordered by God – how can you set the word against dreams – visions – angelic messengers – put them in a cage and expect one to defeat the other – The contradiction is clear, the word and the acts of God are one and the same – Much of the scripture's content is of these dreams –

visions – messengers of God – You can not separate them or deem one more important than the other – I realize my perspective may seem extreme in proportion to what was actually preached like I am simply over reacting or reading to far into it –

However I feel responsible to report that which is discerned –

It may not be evident to everyone when looking at the words alone but to me we put these things secondary and even of no importance - being more cynical and apprehensive then excited and welcoming to the Holy Spirit and His gifts – Paul concludes his letter saying *"earnestly desire and set your hearts on prophesy and do not forbid or hinder speaking in Tongues"*

I conclude with my main concern - that this instance has followed a trend of comments that reflect a doctrinal view and or personal preference of the pastors that should not be embraced by the assembly but rebuked.

SOME OF THE CHURCH

[*some of*] the church is allowing itself to be led by a political sect, causing themselves to seem as a part of the world as we know it- the conservative party- WE ARE NOT THIS PARTY,,, we are a kingdom, The Kingdom of God- **the problem in choosing a party is that the party will fail in reflecting who WE ARE**, a party may have a few principles in common but will also lack in a few that the opposing party may have, in putting yourself exclusively at the whim of one party you send a message to unbelievers; a message that invites the world to define Us, when really I would like to surprise an unbeliever to the power and love of God, bringing him to submission- **We are Christians**, greater than all parties; I do not say this in a spirit of vanity (do not be deceived) but by His authority whom has put our hand to the plow- **if WE do not snatch others from the fire WHO WILL?** It has been put on US to bring man to deliverance, this is the most important task in the universe, the most pressing, most noble, virtuous policy we can have.

This is our policy, no other party shares in this pursuit and yet we do not draw unity from this, no; we aim to become associated with a passing political party simply because we think they have the power to secure our hopes and dreams from becoming our fears and nightmares- with all respect; turn, repent and forget this vain trust. **Admit we have found ourselves upset, angered and determined,** NOT in sustaining our war against darkness BUT in sustaining what we think is our place in this culture war, this fight to get a conservative into the office we hold in such foolish glory, as if they receive omnipotence with their office- this fight to bring conservative ideals into the law books and federal mandates of America; We know there are laws and we do not have to depend on man to uphold them, we do not need to depend on the supreme court, it is not as supreme as those He has called to judge, *do you not know we will judge angels,* do you not know there are Thrones and Books; all the deeds of man are kept in perfect accuracy by Him- Let him who does evil continue in doing evil and those who do good continue in doing good,

His justice will prevail without the kings of the nations and So Be It-

"LIVE LIFE WITH A DUE SENSE OF RESPONSIBILITY, NOT AS THOSE WHO DO NOT KNOW THE MEANING OF LIFE BUT AS THOSE WHO DO"-

POLITICS

For a while now I have been watching and learning from an ever changing political climate;

in searching for clear distinctions among unclear denominations harvesting unclear relatives of thought, I would like to coin a term to better describe who it is I speak of- pupilles of licentia.

These who I am speaking actually have my utmost concern at ransom, so, I am not one more spouting his point of self interested resent. Those who I have zeroed in upon are those which have been born again, it is my brothers and sisters that I am judging and not the world. Along the way I have learned very much of each fickle debate, they move along so fast to and from certain ravings without even the least bit of worry that it could all be said for not, or that there may be a worthy refute. Without a conversation me and very, very few have no choice but to look closer at any given accusation but without the company of the accuser. To better define these I will state; they are both rigid and conservative and yet panicky in their demands for a more libertarian like approach to social dilemma- they seem to distance themselves from social injustice yet will fight against laws that will allow such things as abortion and stem cell research and immigration and so on, that is... today at least, it changes by the day- but worst there is such a spirit of anger and fear obviously percolating from their hearts- says me. They seem sure of who they are... amazingly sure, I however am no longer sure who they are. I am perplexed, baffled, seriously bewildered, maybe I think too much, question too much, maybe I give one too many fair shakes to an issue, whatever the case, this is a very crazy manifestation of political- cultural hatred; almost smells racist. Perhaps that is just me trying to figure out the great Christian passion focused against a standing president, against a standing campaign and against their own beloved democracy- yes against democracy. So my focus or ability to judge lies within the Christian perspective, if you get my drift, if you do... good, you still speak the language. So onward with the clause-

To you- the American Christian, the pupilles of licentia – Actually I first would like to say thank you to the few who even though may not like what is happening with the country's political affairs are still able to have a real dialogue, a real life, honest conversation, you are beautiful stoic princes, thank you. What I love of these brave beating brains is that when a truth is discovered they fearlessly face it whether it compounds with their ideal or not, in the words of the Jewish physicist " The right to search for the truth implies also a duty; one must not conceal any part of what one has recognized to be the truth".

It is they that keep me even searching in order to reveal- even though the sorrow of seeing so many so called Christians rising up under this carnal ideology is at times enough to fall into dark depths of human depression. Having an argument of factual materials would be one thing but that is not what we see, why, because an ideology needs no truth, the spirit of this battle is so chaotic so unorganized so angry it leaves those who do not share the same emotion simply alienated. The reason for their aggressive declarations is due to a fearing heart and one who has lost its substance.

Here is the point where I will attempt to be specific in the hope that some may lose the heavy and uncomfortable scales from their eyes; in the old books of the scripture we say we love and adore so greatly you will find a God who sees and cares of the poor, the sojourn. He sets laws in order to provide for these who have not, now I do not want to be overly simple BUT I think simple will help bring this all to a simmer; we are to understand that we are also sojourners, as he said to the Jews "you too were once strangers in a foreign land. This country we find ourselves in, of all countries is the capitol of the world- the melting pot, all of us besides those natives in which the countries founding fathers drank of their very lives are from elsewhere... our ancestors came from another piece of earth across the seas that once separated territories, how so many wish there were a great sea between tis of thee and Mexico- It is of you,. Are we now greedy with The Beautiful? Is it now ours? Look this is a democracy , the people vote and the outcome are those in power, some say that means were in power, some say the government does what they want,, either way the Christian is now upside down, before it was "submit to the governing authorities" now... well do I even need to say how the Church has reacted to the president, his party- be honest, think about it- I do not even know what to do with today's Church, for they do not know what to do with themselves, no it seems you are now some sort of freedom soldiers- it truly is difficult to rouse the hearts of God's Church to activate the Spirit within them to radicalize their life, AND now how easily their hearts are seduced with revolt for the cause of the constitution, the country, the godly republican party, the founding fathers, blah, blah, blah- you can claim to be defending but who do you think you are kidding, the offensive is where many of you are, the offensive in the war of... perhaps saving what you think is your country, your nation under god.

THE MACHINE TO COME

We ARE driven by the status quo, by industry, by the mere act of ridicule we would need to endure by refusing the pace of the rats racing to a grand almighty dollar. You can claim a balance but what balance is there, and if such a balance is somehow possible, somehow struck by today's "Christians" it is some magical unseen truth, unable to distinguish us from the world; I am sorry as an apologetic- truly sorry. You can not serve both God and mammon. Let us just be honest; admit we are not in the right place, the right condition, the Church has made its way through history to settle into a sterile position within humanity as simply responsible adults- someone, anyone can count on. We are the only people who do not see the sense in being as radically different as our leader- No, making something of ourselves is much more important, I have seen and heard of those who willingly accept the cold fact; it is for money they have been shot, stabbed, gone without food fueled by coffee into each new day and night of enterprise, focused, reliable, determined..... for the boss- except there are side effects, contradictions within the soul do not just lye dorm it; our bodies are manufacturing stations for sure, progress is made for the ambitious, goals are met, masters award promotions; demanding more.... leaving us no choice but to rise in our successes, proving true a man's capacity to love, to betray, to serve- Just Look at the cities of man, the ports, highways, towers, and the innumerable structures of commerce,,,, do we really think these were all constructed for the glory of God; do we really think that the notion;;;" where would we be without these wonders" will carry us to the almighty TRUTH of the matter; OF THE SPIRIT- the history of industry is there to analyze, the history of empire even worst- I understand the struggle brothers, the difficulties of this matter, still, it was not intended to be a compromise, was not intended to be the easy way- I will state most confidently; the worst thing to ever happen to God's child was Capitalism, for this has given merit to the struggle of finance.... it is this who makes Carl Marx; his manifesto a thing of prophetic utterance; for even he saw the certain loss of mystic Christian fervor on account of the Machine to come.

SUBMIT INSTITUTION

This chapter; really verse 13- seems to some enough reason to "let official men be their guide" at least that's how I discern the spirit that asks how it is that I can go on breaking tradition after reading this verse..... Well let's take a close look-
English Standard Version 1 peter 2 -

"Be subject for the Lord's sake to every human institution, whether it be to the emperor as supreme, or to governors as sent by him to punish those who do evil and to praise those who do good. For this is the will of God, that by doing good you should put to silence the ignorance of foolish people. Live as people who are free, not using your freedom as a cover-up for evil, but living as servants of God. Honor everyone. Love the brotherhood. Fear God. Honor the emperor. Servants, be subject to your masters with all respect, not only to the good and gentle but also to the unjust. For this is a gracious thing, when, mindful of God, one endures sorrows while suffering unjustly. For what credit is it if, when you sin and are beaten for it, you endure? But if when you do good and suffer for it you endure, this is a gracious thing in the sight of God. For to this you have been called, because Christ also suffered for you, leaving you an example, so that you might follow in his steps. He committed no sin, neither was deceit found in his mouth. When he was reviled, he did not revile in return; when he suffered, he did not threaten, but continued entrusting himself to him who judges justly. He himself bore our sins in his body on the tree, that we might die to sin and live to righteousness. By his wounds you have been healed.

For you were straying like sheep, but have now
returned to the Shepherd and Overseer of your souls"

Also together with verse thirteen the entire writing of James
and the second letter of Peter go especially well with the
understanding.... if you have the time... if not you can just pick a
doctrine that sounds most popular... but I wouldn't do that.!

The basis is lost when focusing on a single verse; basically a
true Christian will not break the laws of man however the law
makers or law givers or enforcers of the law *will sometimes break us-
even though we have done no wrong and the verse immediately states that
within its context.*

The laws of civic decency were given by God, inserted into
the conscience of man; we all want to be treated fairly... don't we.
Except these Holy Scriptures assure us we will not be BUT count it
as joy when the world or the institution of man persecutes you; for
our Lord our Savior also suffered in this way.

It is not man's way in which we follow or the world's
government that we are directed but unto righteousness- a much
higher way, one that does not truly offend man's law- just as Christ
laid out this fact: that by loving your neighbor you sum up the law-
one who loves his brother breaks no law against him not one,,, for
he loves him.

Man's law is always changing therefore it cannot be said
that it is perfect or eternal- and at times throughout the ages
man's law has turned against Gods people making it illegal to do
what God commands- Babylonian, Roman, German, China,
Russia- and on and on and on- within the Acts Of The Apostles
I am inspired at the courageous dialog between Peter and the
High priest the Apostles and the council: WE MUST OBEY
GOD RATHER THAN MEN. And sometimes that is exactly
what it comes down to, and that can be seen throughout the
scriptures,, throughout the life of the man of God. So choose
you this day whom you should serve. Paul stood before Agrippa,
before Caesar; Jesus spoke of those who would follow Him... He
said "do not think of what you will say but the Holy Spirit will
come upon you when you stand before kings and governors, you
will be beaten in synagogues.

The point is to realize that the urge to be overly interested in supporting a human political system is impure and off base. The Christian has an even higher standard to abide by.

Before the word institution in verse 13 is *human* which together: **human institution** in the original Greek translates to-HUMAN CREATION.

PERSONAL POLITICO

Personally- One having the right to think, to cast a view, to cast a vote, to act confidently according to his or hers own conscience. One in a majority how else could it be, yet to unite is a leaders cry, unite, unite, unite, and the people search the leader for direction; unite for what, they quietly ask themselves hoping to figure it out by watching others and having the complexities of overlapping variables simplified for there's no time for due study. I have seen pawns gathered against kings in a land where issues are separated only for votes and men are mere figures of an American ideal, give the people what they want in word and you choose the majority's desire, they choose you and you gain the power- congratulations to you kings of the earth you have done it, you have been accepted in presidential grandeur, your identities have been staked in human popularity and your shadow will be known by all people and yet still only a passing shadow. You as world leader in this age of man have chosen the wrong way there is no reversing the motion, the vacuum,, still you promise change., you try solving the causes of unhappiness and unrest with civic adjustments, this is not the Gospel but government- Greece fell and with it Rome -The Platonic order, The Republic- none protected man from mankind ,you poor and pathetic people who has bewitched you- supporting man and his kingdoms when the Gospel has been revealed to us and with it its King, we are not citizens here, let the daddy war bucks- baby boomer's- x- y- upper- lower management all go to hell where it's headed, let any ideal any knowledge that places itself above the knowledge of God – I am the enemy of the state that has attacked The Bride- trying to make fools of my brothers and sisters, trying to call the Church their own trying to use us to achieve their own gains- why do you all follow behind waving flags, choosing for yourselves the best man when neither are best, there is no best, you're playing the world's game by the world's rules,-" are looking for a king to produce a godly democracy,"- come on, you're voting on one issue, one party, one side against another until you get so wrapped up with it you preach their sermon; leave them to their own realm and be a fisher of men. Why so strongly promote a man whom you do not know, when the Apostle Paul spoke with officials he worked to persuade hearts for the salvation of souls, we are the ministers free from the law, given all things to do such work, the political arena is not the Church and you have had your senses betrayed by fear and love of this world; yes wanting the world to conform to our standard without accepting the Son is a twisted ministry- vainglory- against the oracles declared on this world, its system is doomed, stop fighting it, your work is not to change the system of man but your neighbor with the Gospel- government was not the force Christ called to build His Kingdom- read the conversation Jesus had with Pilate, read it slowly and consider carefully the differences between the two men, the two perspectives, the two truths of two kingdoms and two kings-

"So Pilate went back again into the judgment hall and called Jesus and asked Him, Are You the King of the Jews?

Jesus replied, Are you saying this of yourself [on your own initiative], or have others told you about Me?

Pilate answered, Am I a Jew? Your [own] people and nation and their chief priests have delivered You to me. What have You done?

Jesus answered, My kingdom (kingship, royal power) belongs not to this world. If My kingdom were of this world, My followers would have been fighting to keep Me from being handed over to the Jews. But as it is, My kingdom is not from here (this world); [it has no such origin or source].

Pilate said to Him, Then You are a King? Jesus answered, You say it! [You speak correctly!] For I am a King. [Certainly I am a King!] This is why I was born, and for this I have come into the world, to bear witness to the Truth. Everyone who is of the Truth [who is a friend of the Truth, who belongs to the Truth] hears and listens to My voice.

Pilate said to Him, What is Truth? On saying this he went out to the Jews again and told them, I find no fault in Him.

But it is your custom that I release one [prisoner] for you at the Passover. So shall I release for you the King of the Jews?

Then they all shouted back again, Not Him [not this Man], but Barabbas! Now Barabbas was a robber."

Here Jesus explains so clearly His Kingdom does not belong to this world AND DONT MISS THIS, *"if My kingdom were of this world, My followers would have been fighting to keep Me from being handed over to the Jews."*

I hope you have mind enough left to discern what that means, realize what age we are in and stop acting like a naive immigrant crossing the sea to streets of gold, America, America, can you let it go?

Can our pastors control themselves enough to withhold their opinion knowing their influence towards the flock- so easily coaxed in which way to vote the Sunday before elections- can our mothers brothers and sisters get used to not being any determinate in saving this sinking ship; making the difference in a realm of indifference, greed, power, and obscurity- not that we lay down the good fight, no, the opposite; you arrogant unlearned pupil... but that we stand up, not as Americans a temporal nation but as the Church as we are, that is our realm, the American evangelicals of the first half of the century didn't even want government in the way, **they wanted** the separation of church and state, let the ax be at the root, let the country fall, let the world judge the world, as Paul states my business is to judge the church not the world, come on make the distinction it's there to see, American history IS forgotten, if you knew it you would wonder how you all became such a tool to the conservative party; Founding fathers, NOT MY fathers, my father is Abraham- my father is God the Father, these American founding fathers you all puppet rejected the divinity of Jesus they were Masons they were the establishments man they could care less for the Church they were about freedom for everyone, for every religion, every habit whether good or bad whatever you please and that is not the Gospel that's America- one American father even sat in the oval office rewriting the New Testament, went to church once a year to appease a wife and refusing to take communion, Washington, Adams- this isn't conspiracy theory this is men, this is science, that was their god, it's documented and it's true you just haven't turned your blind eye to see for yourselves, to see through the veil of your day but rather you support a most modern political party- instead of loving the truth of every matter- HERE'S MY PARTY ... The Bride of Christ AND MY FIGHT, for The King, He is coming.

TO THE CHURCH NEW LIFE

The year started with a group of young adults sharing their lives together, for a certain few, it was every day. This lifestyle brought out the best and the worst in one another as it seems was the Holy Spirits plan exactly. We would cook food and eat together, read and listen to scriptures, play instruments and sing, but probably the greatest thing was when someone was perplexed, upset or just off course. There would be gained the attention of the entire squad. There really were all the parts of the church in our little group. There were teachers, caregivers, encouragers, and all kinds of hints and leadings of the Holy Spirit. The brother or sisterhood became the backbone of each one's individual commitment to Christ (Since we are surrounded by so great a cloud of witnesses- Hebrews 12:1). The pressure to choose wisely was just right, even though a few gaskets blew from time to time, and in this experience iron certainly sharpened iron. Discoveries of deep spiritual importance were made, be sure of that. Most of the time we spent together was in a home or an apartment; we spent more time together there then in a church building or in public combined, if you choose to draw any conclusions from that fact. Outreach mostly consisted of many attempts to enlarge the group by bringing others in, whether they were loaners or couples that stuck closer than brothers, and I would say we succeeded to a degree at which we did not always remain comfortable. When going into public one or two at the least would proclaim good news to unbelievers, at least on one occasion we were used to call one back from falling away. There were short stints with other churches, there seemed to be a reoccurring realization of how long of a bridge would be needed to pull random assemblies close. Yet some flourished in other places and were named a blessing, we hoped to give New Life a reputation for this. Yet God has control of the church's direction (A man's steps are of the Lord; how then can a man understand his own way? -

Proverbs 20:24). Looking back through the year, you could easily deduce that we have come up short, and if looked at with only a glance, its true the group as it was is no more. However that would be an incomplete teaching, as much as I would like to say that everyone who was a part is only separated because of a calling that has put distance between us, I must not give way to this sentiment. For some, their journey has led them elsewhere for reasons that are not clear and others for reasons that should be left undeclared, for their path is their own and we are only being placed in different seasons of their lives, some, even in the first of being born again, "so let us not define each other's reality"; they are yet alive and loved by God. Now for the ones still here at New Life, we have not of recent times but for a time longer integrated ourselves closely to members of all ages and gender, seeing our impact as important and our relationships strong, so let us not grow weary of doing good, we are seeing in my opinion a very great movement happening within the church, this group the young men and women presently attend is a diverse gathering with huge evangelistic potential, just ask anyone who gathers there and I'm sure they will be full of wonderful things to tell you. So the group is and will be. Furthermore, no one should be discouraged, for the Lord is the one who entrusts us with each other and He will be the one who invest more into our lot. (Whoever can be trusted with very little can be trusted with much, and whoever is dishonest with very little will also be dishonest with much.-Luke 16:10). As for further defining the group that is, I relent, for it is a beautiful painting not yet comprehended.

ENTER MY REST

The Book Of Hebrews has in chapter four showed in Holy Words a reality that I often attempted to articulate- with these verses in chapter four my thoughts have been confirmed as truth and also fulfilled- added to and completed-

Therefore I am convinced and am a believer in this truth: Many believers enter the gateway to the way- to the hard and the narrow- they begin just as they are with the passage of Grace-

Beginning but failing, in failing to shed the labors of the old self they fail to enter His rest_ which is the completion that Christ has produced through His works for us- and for us to rest- for us to lean- to trust, solely on God_ the Gospel of Jesus Christ to men. Amen. What we have is a people willing to show homage by outward practice of religious routine but fail to give up all human effort to let God be God- the aftermath of this sort of failure is worry, anxiety, dread, guilt, regret, resentments and insecurities in all parts of life- this is summed up in these words: "They Shall Not Enter My Rest."

Does God withhold His Rest after offering it to us, or do we refuse to accept it in replace of our own feeble acts to secure our expectations- so choose to serve God or self- self will be restless while God permits rest and LIFE-JOY to His servants. Amen.

Thank you Holy Spirit for in meditation you show my spirit that all is well and complete for You Have Overcome the world-

THE TEACHERS MOUNT

Not many of you should be teachers.

First let's clear our mind of our own concepts of exactly what a teacher is. Now that we have done this open your mind to perhaps a more biblical view. Let us begin with Jesus our Lord.

A teacher is one who knows truth and speaks it; this is a good teacher a false teacher speaks falsehood. Careful consideration of the book of James chapter three surprising parallels the

Pharisees introductory description of just what sort of teacher Jesus is. "Teacher, we know that you are true and teach the way of God truthfully, and you do not care about anyone's opinion, for you are not swayed by appearances." This is the model of a true teacher, truthful unwavering to popular belief and impartial to things seen - a man walking in faith to the spoken word of God and attesting to it – We have so many excessive opinions in the church shaped by many influences outside the holy scriptures – Jesus spoke scripture taught scripture corrected with scripture and when acted in divine power complimented not contradicted, fulfilled not abolished the rulings of the almighty God – He was sent from above knowing and leading in all righteousness, His context every context set before Him and in these He masterfully set the record straight one by one *and they were all astonished!*

This is the very vehicle we are now going to allow to take us up the sermon's mount – Could you see them all – all of them around Him this carpenter's son with this keen sense of right and wrong making it seem all so obvious to them - He wouldn't struggle it was all there, it was all known to this teacher - when others studied the law and copied it from one parchment to another He would find solitude and speak to His Father and listen; carrying out every step of the plan that was prepared by them before the very foundations of the earth. He was a perfect man never offending in speech with error- not by avoiding social intercourse to the contrary engaging in it – With each question amounting on the last the Pharisees must have thought He was bound to lose to one, become stumped and say something foolish, this radical that drinks with the destitute, defiling Himself with lawless company, exchanging words with society's extorters whose scales exchange unjust sums - loving the unlovely – As their attempts seemed only to produce more hateful jealousy they could only wait in desperation for an opportune time to overthrow this prophet who had the heart and minds of the people and rightfully so –

His disciples leaned hard on their master - they were sharing in prophetic fulfillment, the coming of the One True Son Of God - this was He and their souls were filled with the hope of salvation, the hope of the greatest leader the world has seen – Living in the present with Living Water they hung on His every word leaving their former lives and the ways of providing for themselves putting trust in this one from Nazareth, they followed Him, inspired, motivated, empowered with the power of Holiness –

As Jesus walked through the towns of Israel He pitched seeds of truth amongst the hearts of all – some seed fell in the process of fulfilling the prophesy of Isaiah; hard tradition grew callused fat dull hearts, eyes tightly closed, ears heavy, they could not breathe this new air they could not swallow just how fresh it really was- this was the grievous condition of the chosen race of God, the ones the prophets cried aloud to- only to be battered with stones and an unwilling cooperation of a nation's wayward heart - they could not perceive – Disclosing pearls of never before heard Holy Scripture He had purpose for them He had dominion to give – Apostleship - *"to you it has been given to know the secrets and mysteries of the kingdom of heaven, but to them it has not been given."*

Those to lead the spiritual revolution- those would not be objects of wrath but instruments for extraordinary purposes to bring the fallen house of Israel and barbarians alike under the Gospel, under the blood of the messiah, to expound on the coming events that would usher in the New Covenant, the New Testament Church, the Church that would be a universal body of believers all linked by a great and powerful spirit THE HOLY SPIRIT- THE SPIRIT OF TRUTH – this is what The Teacher was preparing His pupils for, His teaching had relevance – timely and timeless- Jesus- teacher-prophet- king- lion and the lamb He would be the all sided man of God – He would teach in the synagogue, He would travel about and

He would stand high and exalted on the mount- Still rather than associating this teacher with a place look more to the condition and the topics in which he operated – Perfection- absolute loving intention- perfectly spoken knowledge, amply uttered turning error into apples set in gold – with each thing spoken a line was drawn between truth and falsity, dividing with a precision light from darkness, bringing to a dull point the sting of death– He was full of light and truth and so shining before men to bring honor and glory to God - full of light and truth this is His condition-

His topics in which He operated was all this talk of God, right and wrong, the law, the afterlife- sin- life and death, reward and punishment, sons of obedience and sons of disobedience – these topics are prevalent today, we hear opinions loud and soft logical and senseless – we see the ones who have a grand stand filling stadium churches with thousands of *FAITHFUL LISTENERS* and those filing down in all degrees to even the one who has left all, leaving even their hair to grow long appearing as a trap of ridicule and shame,- this one thing binds them together for the judgment - they all have their words- bringing them to the places they go to reveal them to sheep to heard them from wolves- Here on the mount we must acknowledge the life we have to live. The people we have to share it with, our person, whatever stage or season we are in and to have the hope and discernment to move forward at the beckoning call towards holiness – Here there is the young the old the wise and the foolish, no matter their outward condition they are on the mount – Some need to be corrected others encouraged the teacher must see the difference and assert sayings accordingly- there is the old view and *the coming enlightenment,* this is especially a sensitive task, to call the ones of the law to a higher sense of being – there's to know – there is to be – the ones who do righteousness and teach righteousness are important to the kingdom -are true- are teachers confident before their judgment – teachers of evil and those who practice wrong doing are least important to this kingdom that will reign forever, there on the mount He heightened the law with love and flew higher then their gauge of the law could read until reaching a place of depths; until reaching the reflection of the human heart – to hate – to begrudge – to lust – to take – if there before the judge you realize wrong within retrace and go seek to be forgiven and return with the invisible visibly clean for the invisible God to see and receive his servant's offering – There on the mount The Teacher simply corrects – updates – and acclaims who it is great before God - This is what it is to be a teacher – it is to be a reprover- a reprover of others – Back to James – not many of you should be teachers- not many of you should be correcting others – not many of us should be self – constituted sensors for you will be judged by a higher standard and with greater severity – *"For we all often stumble and fall and offend in many things. And if anyone does not offend in speech [never says the wrong things], he is a fully developed character and a perfect man, able to control his whole body and to curb his entire nature."*

Jesus was this perfect man and with all his teaching all His correcting He was found blameless never saying the wrong thing – still think again all those words all those questions – those futile attempts to ensnare Him in His words and still not a single fault –

He went to death a perfect man being judged by God a worthy sacrifice for our great many offenses – for this perfection God raised Him from this sacrificial death and He was given to an indestructible life

TO JESUS A PERFECT TEACHER
GIVEN TO AN ETERNAL PRIESTHOOD
YOU ARE A PRIEST FOREVER AFTER THE ORDER OF MELCHIZEDEK
MY LORD GIRD MY LIPS WITH KNOWLEDGE FROM ON HIGH THAT I WOULD LEAD WISELY AND NOT OFFEND THE TRUTH
GIVE ME DISCERNMENT TO KNOW WHAT WORD TO SEND FORTH INTO THE BATTLE OF GOOD AND EVIL
SHOW ME MY WRONG THAT I MAY BE LIFTED FROM IT SO TO PLOW FORWARD
OVERSEE MY WORK THAT I MAY STAND BEFORE YOU ON THE DAY OF MY JUDGEMENT

REFRESHING THE HEARTS OF THE SAINTS

We find in Philemon a bond between Paul an Apostle of Christ Jesus and every other believer mentioned in the book-it's an inspiring glimpse at the early church- their fellowship was galvanized with the work of spreading the gospel- this was not just good works but a burden of burning passion to preach Jesus the risen Lord to all with the power of the promised helper the Holy Spirit- proclaiming the good news they found adventure together- they experienced how dedicated God was to their lives as they gave all of themselves to bringing forth His eternal Kingdom- Paul speaks of his heart- I am sending him back, sending my very heart- how did Onesimus become Paul's heart what type of relationship brings forth such a poetic line-I am sending him back sending my very heart- as Onesimus went from one standing to another, with Philemon a slave- with Paul a dear Son- Paul's life as an Apostle meant a passion for the church- new believers and steadfast servants alike-his commitment led him into love with fellow workers man and women- in the greeting he says my fellow soldier and fellow worker to the church in your house; these people were submerged completely in the cause of spreading the gospel- and while so doing forming bonds with one another that are defined militantly- fellow soldier, fellow worker- there's a certain intensity to a relationship between people that share in difficult or stressful situations-old war buddies are linked by events only they can recall together, some horrible others extremely relieving or refreshing- fellow workers –when at work your workmates are the ones who can sympathize with you and relate to the day to day tasks they also take up much of your social element on a weekly basis- some annoy and make a difficult job harder- some relieve and we are glad to accomplish things with such a person, when we make a mistake they catch it, when we become tired they pick up the slack-

they relieve us they refresh us "they refresh our hearts" verse 7 gives the first amazing exaltation-For I have derived much joy and comfort from your love, my brother, because the hearts of the saints have been refreshed through you. Paul says that he has derived much joy and comfort, and why- because the hearts of the saints have been refreshed through you- So Paul being so involved genuinely felt joy and comfort when the saints hearts were refreshed- Paul said comfort- comfort. Not stressed out- He was a slave unto Jesus and the only thing as good as taking care of the kingdom was seeing and hearing of other people taking care of the kingdom, taking care of all his hearts all his loves his children his fellow workers –fellow soldiers-now after this affectionate profession Paul states his authority, he stated who he was. Paul the apostle knew his role and states- I could command you to do what is required verse 8-but he says for loves sake I'd rather appeal to you-why; because it was all a matter of love even though he could have ordered it Paul saw this was not in line but instead he showed his love to Philemon and with gentleness he explains his wonderful experience with Onesimus he opens up his heart to his brother Philemon and tells him- I became his father in prison I would have liked to keep him with me even to serve on your behalf. Even though we may know our position in the body just as Paul we must keep in love, we must share with one another, this is the root of our faith-Christ commands- That ye **love one another**; as I have loved you, that ye also **love one another**. Paul says for love's sake I appeal to you though I could command you I appeal- so that that which you will do will be done out of a sincere heart- this would be good for us to observe- to ask one another to keep the standard- gently encouraging towards mutual edification so that all that is done is pure and a true gift to God not a superficial chore unto man-Paul is secure in the hope that his brother will choose justly in verse 21 he says, perfectly confident in your obedient compliance, knowing you will do even more then I ask-Paul did not want his brother to choose because of his own cunning or strength rather he trusted that the sane spirit which is in all who believe would guide and complete Philemon to accomplish this-let us trust not in ourselves with one another but our Father who is over each of us who has perfect wisdom and concern for each situation-Paul writes of his heart, open for the church to read of his love-this act is motivating enough and places the need right on Philemon's heart for God to intercede with approval and unction-Paul explains how useful Onesimus had become to ministry and pleads that Philemon will receive him back as a beloved brother charging Paul for anything owed – Paul pleads give me this benefit refresh my heart in Christ-this refreshing means to make exempt take ease like sit down relax I'll take care of this one-let us refresh one another hearts making the return to the new testament church of fellow workers sharing in passion for both the loss and gains of the Church.

NEWLY WEDS

To those who are newly weds or who may not understand the purpose of such writing-

THE CONTEMPLATIVES- my hope and vision, for a thoughtful generation- sincere seekers of Truth and of Light.

With a burning passion and need for purity and rehabilitation; rehabilitation for the Church- for it is not comparatively as it once was and would do well to strive for the characteristics it once displayed - this is truth to he who allows the scriptures to teach him. For the rehabilitation of the individual in Christ who must be convinced in his own mind of the temporal setting in which he finds himself, thus being no longer conformed to this world and its ways; in this manner, this Man separates himself in a way unlike his former generation- clearing his mind and literally entering into God's rest- this is certain truth to he who allows the scripture to teach him and he who allows the Ghost to compel him to the deeper things of God.

These writings are intended purely for the good and revitalization of the heart and mind, leading to the salvation of souls.

The effort is to invite us all to think again and again and again and again and again...... of God-

For it is my taught belief that such thinking will make us pure, if we search for Him we will find Him, If your mind is steadfast you will be made whole in peace. The Contemplatives are objective thinkers with only one standard and rule, THE WORD- All insight and information is tested by this sword.

The Contemplative joyfully admits there is much to discover, much to debunk and wishes to be the instruments of sound soulful searching and revealing-

The stimulation of the intellect is not equally remarkable with all, however I myself have heard enough discouragement and unfulfilled expression from an extraordinary select, these are the outcast, the prophets freaks and poets,, these do not wish to form a new denomination, no these do not delight in denomination at all but rather would like to further the Kingdom, not separate but in fellowship, in togetherness... many have gone before us in this way- this continues on as a legacy of those who simply challenged one another; now this act of testing is seen as close to evil within the evangelical campaign, there is no tolerance for such, those who dare to question are stigmatized as quarrelsome and accused of causing divisions,, therefore the very virtues of discernment and weighing out have been canonized- words and phrases have since replaced good reasoning as a lukewarm treaty between that which is known and that which is unknown-... this disgusts us.

So then the wish and the momentum is made clear; to further the interest, the passion, of the Church in knowledge and outpouring; to compel and intrigue the unbelieving, so to begin a real quest for the Divine, saving their very selves from a temporal fruitlessness and the loss of eternal enlightenment-

The True Church is not any and every building of peoples on a Sunday, claiming Christ as we know it ,post Reformation (all protestant denominations) ;;no, and if you just stopped and thought about it.... that would become clear- the church is every True Believer gathered; two, four, fifty or one hundred, in a house, a hall or under the willow tree- Monday on through; any thought against this gospel truth should be taken captive for the will of Christ, not your will or your pastors or to the will of your culture.

We do not know what this next century will bring, we do not know how much man will force us to change the ways we look at these institutions; but we should know beforehand how the holiness of scripture defines us- not as Church but as The Church. WE do not believe Sunday worship is in any way wrong, no not at all; we believe the complete truth comes from the Scriptures, deeming every day holy and able to contain Sabbath. This means there is no wrongdoing for he who differs-

LETTER TO THE GROUP THAT CARES

It has been some time since the day we first assembled as "care group" I like many of you have been through quite a bit since- the path I have chosen, or the Lord has chosen for me (whatever you would like to believe) has not been an easy one and it shows no sign of becoming easier, on the contrary it seems to become harder- well, what are you going to do, I will take the low road and you will take the high road, no really, I remember being asked to write a sort of summary for 2007- it started as follows:

"To the Church, New Life- The year started with a group of young adults sharing their lives together, for a certain few, it was every day."

It ended however with this:

"Now for the ones still here at New Life, we have not of recent times but for a time longer integrated ourselves closely to members of all ages and gender, seeing our impact as important and our relationships strong, so let us not grow weary of doing good, we are seeing in my opinion a very great movement happening within the church, this group the young men and women presently attend is a diverse gathering with huge evangelistic potential, just ask anyone who gathers there and I'm sure they will be full of wonderful things to tell you. So the group is and will be. Furthermore, no one should be discouraged, for the Lord is the one who entrusts us with each other and He will be the one who invest more into our lot. (Whoever can be trusted with very little can be trusted with much, and whoever is dishonest with very little will also be dishonest with much.-Luke 16:10). As for further defining the group that is, I relent, for it is a beautiful painting not yet comprehended."

The original letter in full is available to anyone who would like to read it. I addressed what I thought the establishment would like to know; simply what they did not know already. I addressed why some have gone away, or rather, that these who have gone away should not be demoralized for seeking, apart from our presence- instead those who remain are more the substance of what could be known and shared with those who wanted the letter. Personally I did not feel the letter really mattered in the confines to which it was announced, I myself found joy and purpose in the group that was coming to be, I was greatly encouraged that God provided me yet another band of brothers.

I really do not want to add very much to this letter concerning the state of the Church or the Care group, I think people have had quite enough of that, except I must say if there is one admonishment that you will bear, I will leave only encouragement there after- I like you all have a voice and a part in the Kingdom and it just does not matter whether I am liked or disliked, I must go on in the Way God has shown me, with or without support, with or without men understanding, so than I must go on- truly I desire to see all peoples find that God and themselves is greater than their estimation, I desire to see them realize that God knows them, loves them and most of all can use them- I desire to see those who have not found a place to serve, to fellowship, to shine,,, find that place amongst brothers of Jesus- I am not anti establishment, I repeat, I am not anti establishment- however Church establishments are too well established and resist the Spirit's creative will; however if an up and coming establishment were to be established in the light of diversity (paired with Truth), it would have incredible evangelistic potential and this is how many begin, with that very motivation to be different; sadly it is lost through a generation. This means much more than I am willing to write to you for some are not even willing to give fair thought to the meaning of my words any longer, I wish not to write in vain but I do wish to offer some type of explanation for those who may find offense to my course of direction, it is for these I have postponed my decision, I do not wish to offend these but I can not serve only them, I must not sit stagnant for the sake of pleasing some, I must trust the greater purpose of our lives... I do not want to become guilty of perhaps the same resentments I know some of you hold against one another, for there is a perverse and twisted teaching, made to look like love or a sacrifice of sorts. No it seems there is mostly a casual, indecent, charade in place to deal with these conflicts, there is little accountability or guidance in this realm of practical need- if something is wrong it is kept quiet instead of exposed and tended to. If someone alienates or accuses it is likely to be overlooked and taboo to be bothered with, or more awkwardly felt as an annoyance to those who may be aware of such a hindrance. This is my admonishment, this alone.

We have seen so many types of men and woman, I have proudly spoke of us to outsiders, I have shown us to be different, the difference to those who want nothing to do with the mundane characteristics associated with many fellowships today, again no disrespect, these establishments serve and that is good- I have seen and heard a great many sincere thinking men and women consider what they believe before unsaved seeking souls, and I have seen these souls trust and accept guidance from us, I am grateful for this, I have seen and heard great divisions mended for the sake of gathering together and this is praiseworthy, I have seen and heard men and women of God deliver profound wisdom in an orderly useful fashion that can be likened to a group of soloists each taking turn, I have seen and heard all these things, you now possess a surplus of wisdom and knowledge, you are teaming with teachers, you have grown, I salute you all.

A poet decides when to speak and this day I shall utter my last word

Arrows shoot through the night lit ablaze to deter my dreams Metamorphosis-

Thoughts wrapped so tight in silk from the most distinguished of worms in the foothills of Whales

Words have been left, abandoned and mistrusted

No one knows what I need more than me and if that weren't true I would be as poor and pathetic as the rest of the American race

I am a Jew and outwardly wasting away- where is my mind today and what is it that I have to give

As simple as a women walking in her beauty which is a divine sculpting, is it not

A piano keyed in the tune of soul

All living breathing works from the hands of life, how the tree bends and creaks against the wind; it is sound,, the sound of what is,, the way of a fox... all profound the personality of such

For man to perceive... and for man to perceive... well there is something- as the physicist notes "the most incomprehensible thing about the universe is that it is comprehensible" and so it is-

And all its mystery that it preserves merely drives us on, as our muse-

Our surroundings and all that they are- person, place, and thing

I am thankful and vow to be patient and kind to thee- striving to understand why we are here together as notes to a melody; a pleasing sound is made when they are aligned-

THE END

truthsurreal@gmail.com